INTERGALACTIC TRAVELS: POEMS FROM A FUGITIVE ALIEN

ALAN PELAEZ LOPEZ

the operating system KIN(D)* print//document

INTERGALACTIC TRAVELS : POEMS FROM A FUGITIVE ALIEN

ISBN # 978-1-946031-72-3
Library of Congress Cataloguing-in-Publication # 2019956496

edited & designed by ELÆ [Lynne DeSilva-Johnson]

This text was set in Impact Label, Minion Pro, Europa, Franchise, and OCR-A Standard.

The cover is a composite image, with noir overtones, considering the dystopic present reality produced around illegality. It was designed/created by ELÆ using Alan's original shadow photographs.

About that project, Alan writes: *"I have been photographing my shadow for 3+ years. The first time I realized that I was creating a shadow archive coincides when I made a zine on dysphoria. Although I can't say that the shadows and my dysphoria are linked, I can say that I was envious at the anonymity of my own shadow. In some way, these shadows also play on the idea that undocumented immigrants hide in the shadows and can never enter the public sphere because if they do, they can face detainment and deportation. My shadows, then, attempt to critically think about Black optics as they relate to body, embodiment, flesh, and enfleshment. The shadows demand light, but hide. The shadows necessitate a body, but do not mobilize the body. The shadow attempts to detach from the body. The shadow refuses mastery over the subject.*

Your donation makes our publications, platform and programs possible! We <3 You.
http://www.theoperatingsystem.org/subscribe-join/

the operating system
www.theoperatingsystem.org
operator@theoperatingsystem.org

INTERGALACTIC TRAVELS:
POEMS FROM A FUGITIVE ALIEN

UNKNOWN

“In the sixteenth century, New Spain—as Mexico was then called—probably had more enslaved Africans than any other colony in the Western Hemisphere. Blacks were present as slaves of the Spaniards as early as the 1520s.”

-Palmer, Colin. “A Legacy of Slavery.” Africa’s Legacy in Mexico: a Legacy of Slavery, Smithsonian Education, www.smithsonianeducation.org/migrations/legacy/almleg.html.

Fragments of Mixtec and Zapotec Territories
drawn by the poet.
Illustration not to scale

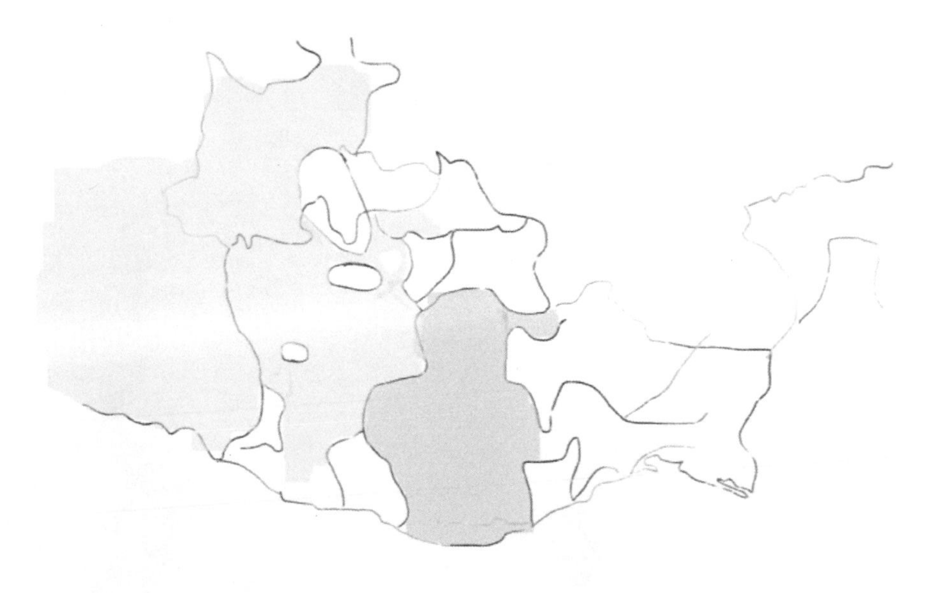

Mixtec

Zapotec

& to think that once, I thought we were lucky
to trace the maps of our names to sailors and warriors.

where you found honor,
we found our owners.

where you found one-third portuguese, two-thirds spanish,
we found one-third NDN slave, two-thirds African slave.

where you found roots,
we found genocidal routes.

& to think that once, I thought we were lucky
to trace the maps of our names to sailors and warriors.

where you found an archive of extraordinary stories,
we found our ancestors kidnapped, transported & enslaved.

where you found romantic cities,
we found occupation, plantations and water pollution.

where you found mestizaje,
we found an attempt at total elimination.

sometimes, I dream of no trans*atlantic slave trade
& I try to imagine no settlement, no last name(s),

no spanish, no dutch, no english, no portuguese, no italian,
no {   }, no {   }, but I do, & I become *illegal.*

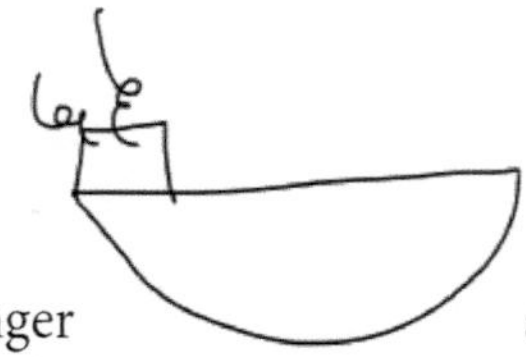

define danger a Black NDN
is kidnapped from their tribe // and chained to the
hold of a slave ship en route to Nueva España

define fear a Black NDN
crosses the San Ysidro-Tijuana border at 5-years-old
they are now an illegal alien // nigger // dead NDN

define worry a Black NDN
never learns Zapotec (as if it were one language)
shaves fro // un-hyphens name // good NDN

define el peligro un Indio Negro
es secuestrado de su tribu // y encadenado a la
bodega de una nave esclava en ruta a Nueva España

define el miedo un Indio Negro
cruza la frontera de San Ysidro - Tijuana a los 5 años de edad
ahora es un extranjero ilegal // nigger // Indio muerto

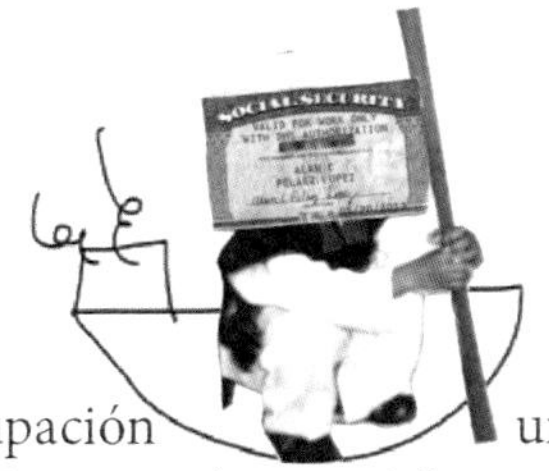

define la preocupación un Indio Negro
nunca aprende Zapoteco (como si fuera una sola lengua)
se afeita su afro, no hifa su nombre, buen Indio

often,
I think about the failure of language:

how does one create verbs
and adjectives to describe terror?;

how does one describe a form of resilience
that requires the magic of
326 different Indigenous communities?;

is there a noun for the type of energy
the *Black* body feels when it senses danger?;

is there an adjective for the type of sex
the *Alienated* wanna have in order to stop time?;

is there a verb for traveling into another dimension
to understand how the *Self* is surviving?;

is there the possibility of being *Human* once again?;

is there a method in which to make sense of life
and remember that after all the violence,
the *NDN* is still an embodied subject
making joy out of all that is supposedly *Dead*?;

is there a glossary for those who have *Arrived*
and have no “home”?;
those who were forced to migrate out of their land?;
and what about those who cannot
remember anything before the *Crossing*?

sometimes, I think about the failure of language:
language once tried to fool me into thinking
that the Black, Alienated, Self, Human, NDN, Dead, Arrivants & Crossers
could not speak.

Language, I do not speak. I scream.

Language,
I do not
speak.
I scream.

UNDOCUMENTED

I certify, under penalty of perjury under the laws of the United States of America, that this application and the evidence submitted with it are all true and correct. Title 18, United States Code, Section 1546(a), provides in part: Whoever knowingly makes under oath, or as permitted under penalty of perjury under Section 1746 of Title 28, United States Code, knowingly subscribes as true, any false statement with respect to a material fact in any application, affidavit, or other document required by the immigration laws or regulations prescribed thereunder, or knowingly presents any such application, affidavit, or other document containing any such false statement or which fails to contain any reasonable basis in law or fact - shall be fined in accordance with this title or imprisoned for up to 25 years. I authorize the release of any information from my immigration record that U.S. Citizenship and Immigration Services (USCIS) needs to determine eligibility for the benefit I am seeking.

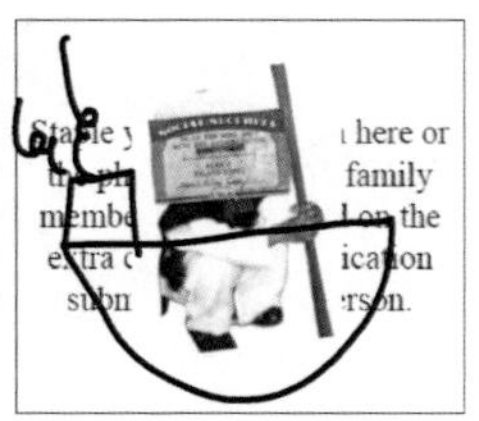

WARNING: **Applicants who are in the United States unlawfully are subject to removal if their asylum or withholding claims are not granted by an asylum officer or an immigration judge. Any information provided in completing this application may be used as a basis for the institution of, or as evidence in, removal proceedings even if the application is later withdrawn. Applicants determined to have knowingly made a frivolous application for asylum will be permanently ineligible for any benefits under the Immigration and Nationality Act. You may not avoid a frivolous finding simply because someone advised you to provide false information in your asylum application. If filing with USCIS, unexcused failure to appear for an appointment to provide biometrics (such as fingerprints) and your biographical information within the time allowed may result in an asylum officer dismissing your asylum application or referring it to an immigration judge. Failure without good cause to provide DHS with biometrics or other biographical information while in removal proceedings may result in your application being found abandoned by the immigration judge. See sections 208(d)(5)(A) and 208(d)(6) of the INA and 8 CFR sections 208.10, 1208.10, 208.20, 1003.47(d) and 1208.20.**

Print your complete name.	Write your name in your native alphabet.
Alan C Pelaez Lopez	you took my alphabet, my language, my people.

BLACK INDIAN CROSSES BORDER AT 5-YEARS-OLD (ZAPOTEC)

I.

-eban -dzuj
-dzuj

II.

-o -dzuj
-dzuj

III.

nyas -dzuj
-dzuj

IV.

tsa's -dzuj
-dzuj

V.

-tahs -dzuj
-dzuj

VI.

tsa's -dzuj
-dzuj

VII.

-znxunj -dzuj
-dzuj -dzuj
-dzuj
-dzuj

BLACK INDIAN CROSSES BORDER AT 5-YEARS-OLD (SPANISH)

I.

despierta   sal'e
          sal ahora

II.

come   sal'e
          sal ahora

III.

vístete   sal'e
          sal ahora

IV.

maneja   sal'e
          sal ahora

V.

duerme   sal'e
          sal ahora

VI.

maneja   sal'e
          sal ahora

VII.

corre   sal'e
          sal'e   sal'e
                    sal'e
               sal'e

BLACK INDIAN CROSSES BORDER AT 5-YEARS-OLD (ENGLISH)

I.

wake up leave
leave

II.

eat leave
leave

III.

dress leave
leave

IV.

drive leave
leave

V.

sleep leave
leave

VI.

drive leave
leave

VII.

run leave
leave leave
leave
leave

WARNING
S-YEAR-OLD
CROSSING
WARNING
S-YEAR-OLD
CROSSING
WARNING
S-YEAR-OLD

Part 1. Information About You (Person applying for lawful permanent residence) (continued)

8. Country of Birth

`"mexico"`

9. Country of Citizenship or Nationality

`unrecognized ndn`

10. Alien Registration Number (A-Number) (if any)

► A- `/ / i l l e g a l`

NOTE: If you have **EVER** used other A-Numbers, include the additional A-Numbers in the space provided in **Part 14. Additional Information**.

11. USCIS Online Account Number (if any)

►

12. U.S. Social Security Number (if any)

► `l o s t a t s e a`

U.S. Mailing Address

Recent Immigration History

Provide the information for **Item Numbers 15. - 19.** if you last entered the United States using a passport or travel document.

15. Passport Number Used at Last Arrival

`no passport: my ancestors were shipped`

16. Travel Document Number Used at Last Arrival

`no documents: all family archives gone`

17. Expiration Date of this Passport or Travel Document (mm/dd/yyyy)

`05/20/1506`

18. Country that Issued this Passport or Travel Document

`is the ocean a country?`

19. Nonimmigrant Visa Number from this Passport (if any)

`no visa: i crossed, alone, illegally`

Place of Last Arrival into the United States

20.a. City or Town

`trad. kumeyaay land`

there is no manual for
Black NDNs whose mothers
have left to the North.
No! forced to the North.
No! {   } to the North.

there is no manual for
4-year-old bois who
are forced into a
dress, locked out of their
caretaker's house, and forced
to stand outside while
other children stare
with rocks in hands:

ready?
aim.
t
hr
o
w!

there is no manual for the
nightmares that haunt the Black NDN
day after day/
after day/ after night/ after
noon/ after night/ after
weddings / after school days/
after date nights / after writing
workshops/ after first kiss/
after last-time-they-see-their-
grandmother/ after making
love /after breaking up /after
eating/ after happiest-day
of-their-week/ after worst-day
of-their-week/ after regular-day
of-their-week.

there is no manual that teaches
Black NDNs to love themselves
past the mental illness that {   }
will refuse{   } caused 'cause
they didn't behave/ 'cause they
should've known better.

there is no manual on how to
block the first rock, and the second
and the third, and the fourth, and
the fifth when the Black NDN is just
a four-year-old toddler
who is being punished in
ciudad Benito Juarez for having been
caught playing with {   },
who is only eight-months-old,{   }
{   } who not yet walks, not yet
uses the restroom, not yet speaks,
but tries to defend
the toddler as{   }cries, and screams
yet is not heard, yet screams,
and is not heard.

there is no manual on surviving
the nightmares, just the
hope that one forgets how
it felt, but not forget how to live,
not forget how to breathe, not forget
how to move, not forget how to walk,
not forget how to dance, not
forget how to laugh.

there is no manual past the
nightmares, so mamá tells me
to write because though she was
not there, she will protect my writing.

so she tells me to write
because though she was not there,

i cannot stay silent.

so she tells me to write
because though she could
not be there, she will protect this thing called *poetry*.

so she tells me to write
because though {   } will never admit what {   }
did, i will have to see {   } every
{   }, i will have to {   } of
{   }, i will have to help {   }
{   }fill
out {   }applications, and
although the nightmares are better
now, i have not finished the
manual because *we* have just
begun writing.

before the crossing[1] our family could understand the whispers of the water[2]. we bathed our cuerpos morenos as if we were holy: as if our humanity was valuable, as if we were worth life. it is hard to remember anything before the crossing[3]. how do i tell myself i had a childhood if at the age of five i am a fugitive[4] of the law? it would be easier to remember life before the crossing[5] if we didn't become paralyzed for the rest of our lives: the doctor tells me i have post traumatic stress disorder. he says it is because i am an immigrant[6], but that in a few years, i will be american[7].

---

[1]during the crossing // we were faced with // the reality // of what it means // to be black and indian // in an empire // that constantly measures us // on production // production // and production. // our blood // a sustenance // for those // who deem us "illegal."

[2]the water here // has been cut through // by wooden logs // that demand // we show them // papers that say // we are not poor // nor indian or black.

[3] i only crossed once // (location: // san diego/ tijuana border // age // five // how // by foot and car.)// but every story heard // becomes another crossing // my body remembers every crossing // every crossing becomes mine // my body has experienced every crossing // in dreams.

[4] fugitive: runaway slave// fugitive: runaway NDN // fugitive: runaway soon-to-be-lynched negro// fugitive: assata shakur // fugitive: mike brown // fugitive: sandra bland // fugitive: alan carlos pelaez lopez.

[5] crossing: the precise location in a five-year-old's life where they lose their humanity, health, and livelihood. // the site where the child realizes their guiding spirit is weakening // the body, changing // the mind, confused // the flesh, shivering // eyes, watering // digits, dancing. // the site where "americans" will blame the child for "infecting" the "american dream."// the site where a child is just a child visiting occupied NDN land.

[6] "the black body does not migrate... it is shipped"- tavia nyong'o

[7] american: i guess i'll be forever "sick."

I am six years-old
and it is Tuesday:

mamá Maria's
only morning off of work

the lower half of my stomach has been hurting for days

I do not tell mamá

I am sure it is another worm
that will make its day-view during a visit to the bathroom

if I am lucky, it won't hurt
I will push my stomach hard when I sit down
until I feel the worm making its way out
and with my right hand, I will pull it out as fast as I can

        (this is how illegal Black NDNs
        take care of themselves)

some of us left home partly because of the plantations
that our family could no longer work in
because all of us kids were dying
and they needed to care for us:
        our lungs too black of pesticide
        our stomachs too fat with worms
        our bodies collapsing from dehydration
                no water for anyone in the village
                though we live on the coast
                but even the gringos own our water

***

I am six years-old
and it is Tuesday afternoon:

my illegal Black NDN body falls to the ground
I wake up to the school nurse telling me

I must go home

mamá Maria works four trains, two buses,
and a twenty-minute walk away

mamá Maria never shows up
          boss didn't let her leave
          (perhaps threatened to report us to ICE)

***

I am six years-old
and it is Tuesday evening:

my first trip to American doctor since the crossing
American doctor yells at mamá Maria in a funny language
mamá Maria yells back in Spanish
I am told to leave the room

outside,
translator comes to me and tells me
not to be scared, (maybe) that there are things
living inside me, that I have anemia
and that I need to eat more

I tell her it's the fruit
and the water
she laughs
tells me I am not
in the Dominican Republic
          (I am not Dominican)
and assures that all fruits
in America are good for me
that all water is clean

I do not believe her

***

I am six years-old

and it is Tuesday night:

mamá Maria disconnects the phone
closes the doors three times,
locks the windows,
& tells me:

cuando tengas que ir al doctor, dime, yo te curo

***

I wonder if the doctor asked for our papers,
probably wanted to know where we come from

maybe she never seen a Black NDN
from North America with a stomach
full of all the wrong things

***

at least she didn't call la migra.

I am nine-years-old
& Mamá Maria tells me que somos negros
I do not believe her
    we have only been in this country for 4 years &
    one thing I know is that only Americans can be Black
    and only Americans can be White
    y yo,
    como puedo ser negro?
    no hablo Inglés, no tengo papeles, mierda no soy Americano

Mamá Maria me dice que somos negros
Mamá Maria tells me that I must learn to love my skin,
    mi piel
    to love my accent,
    mi acento
    to love my culture,
    mi cultura

I do not understand

one year later, bilingual education ends
    (I am shipped to a school 13 miles away)
        (I am labeled Haitian)
        (I am yelled at in French-Creole by an ESL teacher to whom I am her only student)
    (*I do not understand*)
            (c'est garçon est tres stupid)
                (she whispers to another teacher)

I do not understand / I do not understand / I do not understand / I do not understand / I do not understand / I do not understand / I do not understand / I do not understand / I do not understand / I do not understand / I do not understand / I do not understand / I do not understand / I do not

that night, I cry in the bathroom until Mamá Maria comes home from cleaning houses
    I tell her I hate my new school
    I hate the way mademoiselle looks at me
    I hate the way kids pull my hair
    I hate being the only immigrant
    el unico illegal

    I can see the water in Mamá's eyes
    "somos negros" Mamá Maria tells me,
    "pero no le puedes decir a nadie de dónde somos
    porque nos deportaran, y si nos deportan,
    por ser negros, nos van a matar."

NINE-YEAR-OLD PREGNANT BOI

i don't think i want to be pregnant,
but it was always nice to pretend
to be a seahorse and carry children in my stomach

and change what i was
who i was,
what i did
why i did, why i was

after all, it was my mom's boyfriend
who taught me that boi seahorses
are the ones that grow the belly and get pregnant

how i miss playing pregnant
seahorse in the shower

and change what i was
who i was,
what i did
why i did, why i was

The Pledge of Allegiance

pledge allegiance to the Flag of the United States of America's ~~Aryan Race~~, and to the Republic ~~of vanished ndians, niggers & illegal aliens,~~ for which it stands, one Nation under God~~'s instructions to settle, steal, exploit~~, ~~ill and rape~~, indivisible, with liberty and justice for all ~~ready to fight back for our plantation states. Amen~~.

I notice mamá Maria
look at me funny
every time I open mi bocota

I know it is because
I lost my accent
tho' gringos sometimes tell me
I slur my words

mamá Maria knows that
tho' she does not understand
the language, she needs no translation

for the people that speak it
are always sad

how ugly this English is

me doy cuenta que mamá Maria
me mira gracioso
cada vez que abro mi bocota

sé que es porque
perdí mi acento
aunque los gringos me dicen que a veces
travo mis palabras

mamá Maria sabe que
aunque ella no entienda
el idioma, no necesita traducción

porque la gente que lo habla
siempre está triste

qué feo es este inglés

it was in 57 Bennington St. Apt. #3
East Boston, Massachusetts, 02128
where tia Viry first whispered
her name:

Michelle.
Michelle.

my dead
sisters' name was *Michelle.*

at seven, this was the discover of my life.

I saw mamá Maria cry
the first time my small mouth whispered her name——

<<MEEE – SHELL>>

<<MEEEESHELL >>

<<MEESHELL>>

***

when we moved to 333 Meridian
St. Apt. #3 / East Boston, Massachusetts, 02128,
I made sure her name moved with us.

so, when tia Viry gifted me a ring for my birthday,
I named the horse on the ring *Michelle,*
and every Saturday after catechism,
I'd put my hands together and pray:

porfavor diosito,
que no hayan
desenterrado a
Michelle.

***

when tio Timo moved in with us,
I begged him to tell me
about Michelle,
anything.

he lied. he lied to me. he lied.
tio Timo told me she was never born.
he lied. I remember a hospital.
was there a funeral? I remember
visiting her—at the cemetery
I rememeber crying because we
could never afford flowers for her grave.

***

and when we moved to 24 Bolton St.
Waltham, Massachusetts, 02453,
tia Carla moved in with us.
again, I asked her to tell me about
Michelle, and she said she didn't know *anything.*

***

4 years later, we moved to 870 Moody St
Apt. #4 / Waltham, Massachusetts, 02453, and
mamá finally told me, but I did not want
to believe her version. it was then that I
wished tio Timo's lies had been true.

I can sm ell the
dough baki ng from one
bridge and a hi ghway away. Us
waiters have had our in-between lunch and
dinner break—the cook s have been working since 7:3 0 ai-
em wit hout stop. On my second shift of the day, I clock in at 5:
32 pi-em—the 70A was late a nd I did not run across the high
way as fast as usual. It is Sat urday, { } of { },
Mamá's birthday: she is in the kitchen of the restaurant ma
king salads. It has been twe lve hours of standing in the sa
me position, arms rapidly moving to the left and to the
right, only meeting when it is time to mix the greens.
Four more hours to go and she can eat. Amá is
ready to faint in front of the guests. To catch
herself, she sneaks a cherry tomatoe into her
mouth even though the doctor has told her that
the restaurant veggies are too acidic for her
gastritis. As soon as I approach the counter, she
'll ask me to refill her diet coke and grab her a roll.
Even though she's the one that makes them, she can't
often be seen eating them. At 11:00 pi-em, we will walk
to the white minivan, Mamá will rub her pointer fingers on her forehead, and pray to La Virgen de Guadalupe. Her black hat, stained in cactus-shaped tomato sauce will come off, and her ponytail will release wild curls covered in the black Pantene hair dye of the month. The key to the van will turn, and she will drive two exits, right turn to get out, sharp, sharp left, and a right. Two miles later, we will be home. She has to work at 8:00 ai-em tomorrow.

mymotherhasneversaidawordtomeabouthercrossingsoiwriteaboutmineinthehopesthatthiswritingcanhelpuscrossintoeachothersarms

HYPER-DOCUMENTATION

HYPER-DOCUMENTATION

HYPER-DOCUMENTATION

HYPER-DOCUMENTATION

HYPER-DOCUMENTATION

HYPER-DOCUMENTATI

HYPER-DOCUMENTATI

HYPER-DOCUMENTAT

HYPER-DOCUMENTAT

HYPER-DOCUMENTATION

HYPER-DOCUMENTATION

Symptoms of Racialized Nausea

Symptom One—Being Brown, or ~~more dangerous~~, Black;
Symptom Two—Walking on the street with headphones------careful!
Symptom Three— Living in the hood, da projects;
Symptom Four—Too much police, too much circulation;
Symptom Five— Police buying girls from your building for sex;
Symptom Six—Daily assaults outside your kitchen window at E.138th;
Symptom Seven—Finding blood all over the blue elevator door and broken Heineken bottles at your apartment complex *(all that's left are the 50 stars)* on Madison Ave.

***

Racialized Nausea (noun), Definition One—

the feeling a Black Boi gets when he
visits a Home Girl in the hood.
At arrival, heart's at ease, it feels like home, but She worried,
She tell em he must not get too comfortable,
a lot has changed.

***

Racialized Nausea (noun), Definition Two—

Falling asleep at ten pi-em,

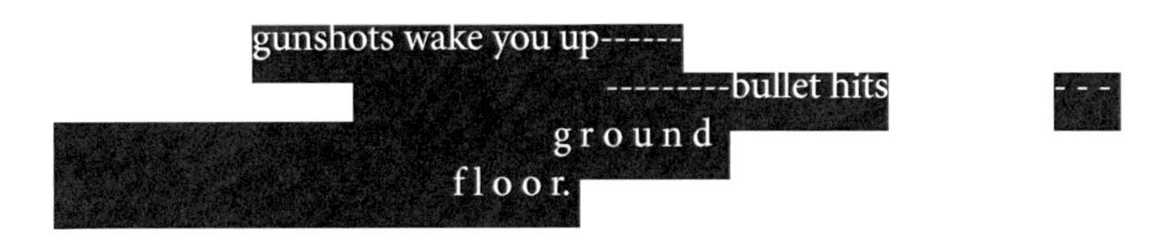

***

Racialized Nausea (noun), Definition Three—

You've parked on the left side of the street,
now you must face what happens to the building at night,
and explain to a 2-year-old that the holes on the wall
are shelters for homeless bees, as you hope
there is no drive-by until you are back inside
{safe}.

***

Racialized Nausea (noun), Definition Four—

The feeling you get after She tell you
no one will hire Her even thought She has papers;
Her address gives it away------------

She not girl who makes it
She not girl who sposed to make it
She not girl with American name
She not girl who should have a career
She not girl who 'worked-for-what-She-has'
She a
[ ].

***

Racialized Nausea (noun), Definition Five—

An obtuse feeling on the stomach
that makes you faint, your body,
hitting the cracked sidewalks that City Hall will not fix
'cause you a problem,
'cause you a commodity,
'cause you Blaq.

***

Racialized Nausea (noun), Definition Six—

a person trying not to drown in organized crime;
a person trying not to buy the coke the NYPD is selling on their break;
a person working 65+ hours a week & still struggling to eat;
a person that seems to still be communal property.

***

Perhaps, Racialized Nausea
is too radical, too academic
how 'bout we call it: blackness embodied?

in under two months, two young bois of color have died and i don't know what to do anymore. joaquin luna jr. was eighteen when he died. the new york times says he committed suicide because he was undocumented. joaquin left a letter detailing the struggles of undocumentedness. this wasn't suicide though, this empire killed him. this empire is killing all of us. i mean, we are here, everyone knows we are here, but the law names us "illegal." technically, we have no rights or legal protection, but at any moment, the law can discipline us; punish us. this is to say that the law selects when it wants to author us into existence. often, i find myself asking: *is there a life after fugitivity, or is fugitivity a way of life?*

***

these have been the saddest days of my life lately. two months and a week after joaquin's death, trayvon martin was killed. trayvon was a seventeen-year-old black boi. in a myfoxorlando interview, his father tells the camera that trayvon was just visiting him from miami. even for those who can legally travel, their travels are met with sequestration and death (but ain't that the story of blackness in the americas? & shouldn't we refuse this story? no longer tolerate *it?*).

***

when joacquin luna jr. died, i was furious and scared — scared that none of us know how to hold each other because we are too busy avoiding our deportations and deaths. when trayvon martin was killed, i felt part of my spirit leave my body and it hasn't returned since. i am tired of reading the news. i am tired of our bodies being documented only after death. i am tired of memorials. i am tired of concerned citizens taking action post death. i'd like all of us to live (please). i want joaquin luna jr. back, i want trayvon martin back. i want the world to love us and hold us.

it's happened again and again and again. i've lost track of how many black folk have died. i kept saving their photos on my desktop. too many photos on my desktop that i kept messing up their names. couldn't put a name to a face anymore. a few looked like me, most were darker than me. a lot were younger than me. *a lot of girls.* i'm scared.

***

i am becoming obsessed with documenting their photographs. they are forgotten so quickly. one of the latest is nia wilson, she was an eighteen-year-old black girl. in an online elegy, her future is spelled out: she was to own a dance studio. days after her death, a friend reminds me that though this violence can happen to us at any moment, the violence hasn't happened to us, and so we hold one another whispering into each other's ear: *i love you, i love you, i love our people.*

***

i keep thinking of trayvon martin and nia wilson's death. i don't know what it is that i'm fighting for at this moment. i use to think that my biggest problem was being undocumented. it's not. i am learning to be black in the united states and it's hard. mamá reminds me that it is also as hard back home because there, we're not just black, but we're the black ndns who survived. and still, amá assures me that the problem isn't blackness or ndn-ness, the problem is the settler's world, particularly settler rage, settler fear, and settler citizenship.

***

i want joaquin luna jr. back. i want trayvon martin back. i want nia wilson back. i want the world to love us and hold us.

extreme dehydration and heatstroke

temperature
reached 101 degrees (38 Celsius)

dehydration

150-mile (240-kilometer)
drive from the Mexican border

dehydration

temperature
reached 101 degrees (38 Celsius)

9 die in
immigrant-smuggling attempt

dehydration

19 immigrants locked
inside a stifling rig

temperature
reached 101 degrees (38 Celsius)

dehydration

nine people
died

dehydration

crammed into a
sweltering tractor-trailer

temperature
reached 101 degrees (38 Celsius)

dehydration

more than 100 people
may have been packed
into the back of the
18-wheeler

temperature
reached 101 degrees (38 Celsius)

dehydration

people died.

I want the world to love us and hold us
I want the world to love us and hold us
I want the world to love us and hold us
I want the world to love us and hold us
I want the world to love us and hold us
I want the world to love us and hold us
I want the world to love us and hold us
I want the world to love us and hold us
I want the world to love us and hold us
I want the world to love us and hold us
I want the world to love us and hold us
I want the world to love us and hold us
I want the world to love us and hold us
I want the world to love us and hold us
I want the world to love us and hold us
I want the world to love us and hold us
I want the world to love us and hold us
I want the world to love us and hold us
I want the world to love us and hold us
I want the world to love us and hold us

NO PAPERS. NO FEAR.
UNDOCUMENTED
MIGRANT
NOSTALGIA
&
BORDERS
NoDAPL
Our Life

INTERGALACTIC TRAVEL(S)
(OR, VIGNETTES FROM AN ILLEGAL ALIEN)

I.

the young person inside me has not visited my dreams lately. perhaps, I have learned to take care of myself, or the little one is tired *(small illegal aliens are tasked with the job to find other galaxies in which to survive and in which to be, maybe I'm there, in the elsewhere).*

II.

I wonder what would have happened if we did not have had to say goodbye to our childhoods *(I am sure some of us had them)* at the moment of running away from fired bullets while crossing the border;

III.

of mounting la Bestia and holding to the roof of a cart for dear life;

IV.

of flying across continents knowing we would never be "home" again;

V.

of driving through immigrant checkpoints pretending to be Amerikkkan;

VI.

of being laid and hammered still inside the floorboard of a boat until we made it to the coast of the states "safe."

VIAJE(S) INTERGALÁCTICO(S)
(O VIÑETAS DE UN EXTRANJERO ILEGAL)

I.

la persona joven dentro de mí no ha visitado mis sueños últimamente. tal vez, he aprendido a cuidar de mí mismo, o el pequeño está cansado (pequeños extranjeros ilegales están encargados con el trabajo de encontrar otras galaxias en las que sobrevivir y en el que estar, tal vez estoy allí, en otra vida extraterrestrial).

II.

me pregunto qué habría pasado si no tuviéramos que despedirnos de nuestra infancia (estoy seguro que algunos de nosotros las tuvimos) en el momento de huir de balas disparadas mientras cruzábamos la frontera;

III.

de montar la Bestia y sostenerse al techo de un carro por la vida sagrada;

IV.

de volar a través de los continentes sabiendo que nunca estaríamos de nuevo en "casa";

V.

de conducir a través de puestos de control de inmigrantes fingiendo ser Amerikkkan@s;

VI.

de ser colocados y martillados dentro de la tabla de piso de un barco hasta que llegamos a la costa del Norte "segur@s".

25¢
AlieN InvasioN
WARNING:
CHOKING HAZARD–Small parts
Not for children under 3 yrs.

Alan Pelaez <alan @gmail.com> 3/17/14

to

Good afternoon

we met in DC this past Saturday morning, where you talked about the different Visas allotted to migrants in the US. I'm the undocuqueer from MA/CT we talked about the T-Visa . I was wondering if you could send me any information about court

Thank you for everything, and have a great weekend,
Alan Pelaez

SOCIAL SECURITY
VALID FOR WORK ONLY
WITH DHS AUTHORIZATION
ALAN C
PELAEZ LOPEZ
USA
05/20/2013

Alan Pelaez <alan @gmail.com> 3/24/14

to

Hello

Thank you for the e-mail and all the information. I just had a meeting with an immigration lawyer that has helped out some of my undocumented friends . She does not believe that will be good for me in court . However, she is calling the clergy to see if some of my traumatic experiences will allow me to enter the court.

Case - Matter of X, No. A , Immigration Rptr. , slip op. at .

I just wanted to see what your thoughts were on all of this.

Thank you,
Alan

Get Paid to Help Find Illegal Immigrants

L <@.org> 3/26/14

to me

You don't want to run out of time. I am out of the office until next week. I would suggest that you find an attorney in NY who can represent you as soon as possible. Good luck! Let me know if you have any other questions! I hope you are having a great day!

SOCIAL SECURITY
VALID FOR WORK ONLY
WITH DHS AUTHORIZATION
ALAN C
PELAEZ LOPEZ
05/20/2013
CAUTIO

You don't want to run out of time.
You don't want to run out of time.
You don't want to run out of time.
You don't want to run out of time.
You don't want to run out of time.
You don't want to run out of time.
You don't want to run out of time.
You don't want to run out of time.
You don't want to run out of time.
You don't want to run out of time.
You don't want to run out of time.
You don't want to run out of time.
You don't want to run out of time.
You don't want to run out of time.
You don't want to run out of time.
You don't want to run out of time.

Find Illegal Immigrants

Get Paid to Help Find Illegal Immigrants

There's a HUGE problem with illegal immigrants

Illegal Immigrant

I hope you are having a great day!

FORMS | NEWS | CITIZENSHIP

Legalize Aliens

How Do

Certain illegal aliens

awful

United States

history

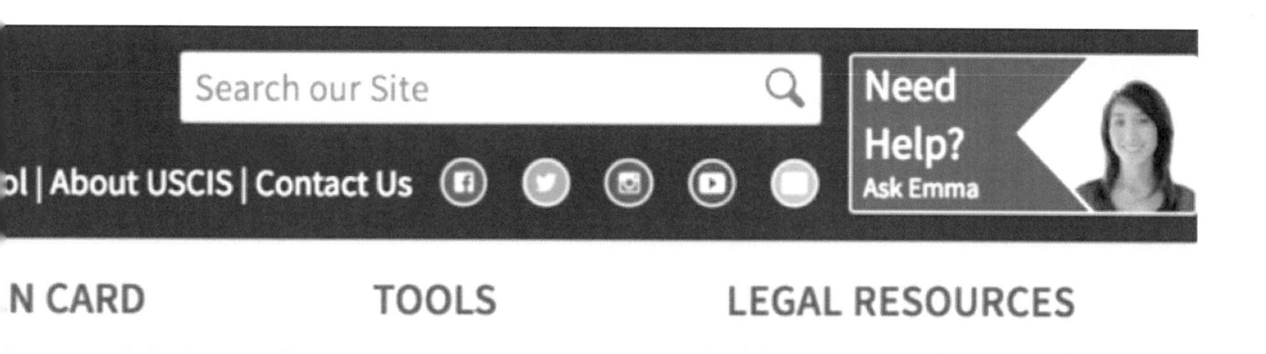
Search our Site
ol | About USCIS | Contact Us
Need Help?
Ask Emma
N CARD
TOOLS
LEGAL RESOURCES

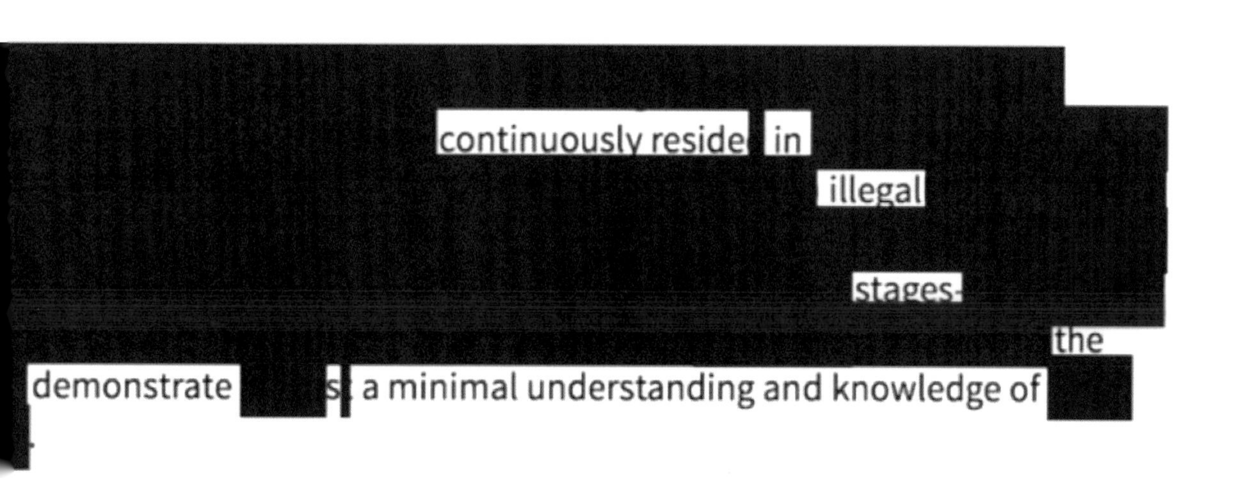
continuously reside in
illegal
stages
the
demonstrate s a minimal understanding and knowledge of

Part B. Information About Your Application

(**NOTE:** *Use Form I-589 Supplement B, or attach additional sheets of paper as needed to complete your responses to the questions contained in Part B.)*

When answering the following questions about your asylum or other protection claim (withholding of removal under 241(b)(3) of the INA or withholding of removal under the Convention Against Torture), you must provide a detailed and specific account of the basis of your claim to asylum or other protection. To the best of your ability, provide specific dates, places, and descriptions about each event or action described. You must attach documents evidencing the general conditions in the country from which you are seeking asylum or other protection and the specific facts on which you are relying to support your claim. If this documentation is unavailable or you are not providing this documentation with your application, explain why in your responses to the following questions.

Refer to Instructions, Part 1: Filing Instructions, Section II, "Basis of Eligibility," Parts A - D, Section V, "Completing the Form," Part B, and Section VII, "Additional Evidence That You Should Submit," for more information on completing this section of the form.

1. Why are you applying for asylum or withholding of removal under section 241(b)(3) of the INA, or for withholding of removal under the Convention Against Torture? Check the appropriate box(es) below and then provide detailed answers to questions A and B below.

I am seeking asylum or withholding of removal based on:

☒ Race	☒ Political opinion
☐ Religion	☒ Membership in a particular social group
☒ Nationality	☒ Torture Convention

A. Have you, your family, or close friends or colleagues ever experienced harm or mistreatment or threats in the past by anyone?

☐ No ☒ Yes

If "Yes," explain in detail:
1. What happened;
2. When the harm or mistreatment or threats occurred;
3. Who caused the harm or mistreatment or threats; and
4. Why you believe the harm or mistreatment or threats occurred.

deoborah miranda says that surviving comes in the retelling / but what does it mean to survive zapotec + mixtec genocide? / slavery? / & illegality?/ how does one quantify the trauma of settler-colonialism? //// at the east boston community health clinic, dr. h laughs at me / when i ask if there is a test for post traumatic slave syndrome. / she looks at me / "imbecile" i read in her eyes, nose, throat & cheeks. //// i want to say the harm, mistreatment & threat is always there: / at the corner store / on the bus / at the y / in my front door / at uc berkeley / at the airport / at the post office. / i want to say that the harm is caused by the settler and the visitor. / i am tired of answering these questions, SIR./ will i live, sir? / do you promise i won't die at the corner store, sir / on the bus? / at the y? / in my front door?/ i am scared, sir / do i pass your test, sir?/ yes, i assure i am a fag, a █████, an ndn.

when
I fall asl eep,
my hands rest on
my heart: afraid that
ICE will come and take everything
from me, the same way the spanish & dutch entered
our ancestral villages and saw our flesh, and wanted our
flesh, so kidnapped, transported, shipped and
auctioned our flesh to/in "nueva españa." and then
came: 1. lemon plantations, 2. papaya plantations,
3. yellow corn plantations, 4. purple corn plantations,
5. bean plantations, 6. banana plantations, 7. coco plan
tations, 8. tamarind plantations, and then came time to
run // to run // to run away from them. and then came the
american whites and: 1. took our coffee beans, 2. and
then the limes, 3. and then the water, 4. and then grand
má unemployed, "no hay más limones que podemos re
coger." afraid immigration will hold a gun in between
my two nipples and ask me for papers, unless I go
back to work for less than minimum wage and stay
quiet when the manager cusses me out in english,
not knowing that I actually understand what he's
saying about "the nigger" as he calls me. and
when I fall asleep, my hands rest on
my heart, amazed at everything my
family has done in el norte,
en los estados unidos
de los jodi
dos.

Over here, as mamá Maria gives me life: hands me a yellow, thin, glowing Ticonderoga (#2) wooden pencil and tells me, "escribe mi'jo, escribe." thankful i can write my own story and remember the smell of eating on a Sunday morning (conchas con cafecito), with the $5.00 "Aló, Mamá" phonecard resting on the mantel, waiting to be used—our family: a settler-empire away.

GOOGLE MAPS DIRECTS ME HOME

a border

away//

a cross away//

a hop away//

a swim

away//

a flight away//

a drive away//

a holler away//

twenty years (and counting) away.

HIGH INTENSITY ENFORCEMENT AREA
OFF LIMITS TO UNAUTHORIZED PERSONNEL
DO NOT APPROACH THE FENCE
AREA DE ALTA VIGILANCIA
FUERA DE LIMITE A PERSONAL
SIN AUTORIZACION
NO SE ACERQUE A LA CERCA

VISION ON THE ELEVENTH DAY OF JULY, TWO THOUSAND FOURTEEN

on
tax-free day
we will   head to
the nine   ty-nine
cent store
to stock up
for the   fall of
this em   pire;
a war that
we win.

l Not Protect Us Papers Wi
l Not Protect Us Papers Wi
l Not Protect Us Papers Wi
l Not Protect Us Papers Wi
l Not Protect Us Papers Wi
l Not Protect Us
l Not Protect Us
Not Protect Us
Not Protect Us
Not Protect Us
Not Protect Us
Not Protec
Not Prote
Papers

ot Protect Us Papers Will N
ot Protect Us Papers Will N
ot Protect Us Papers Will N
ot Protect Us Papers Will N
ot Protect Us Papers Will N
ot Protect Us Papers Will N
ot Protect Us Papers Will
ot Protect Us Papers Will
ot Protect Us Papers Will
ot Protect Us Papers Will
ot Protect Us Papers Will
ot Protect Us Papers Wil
ot Protect Us Papers Wil
ot Protect Us Papers Wil

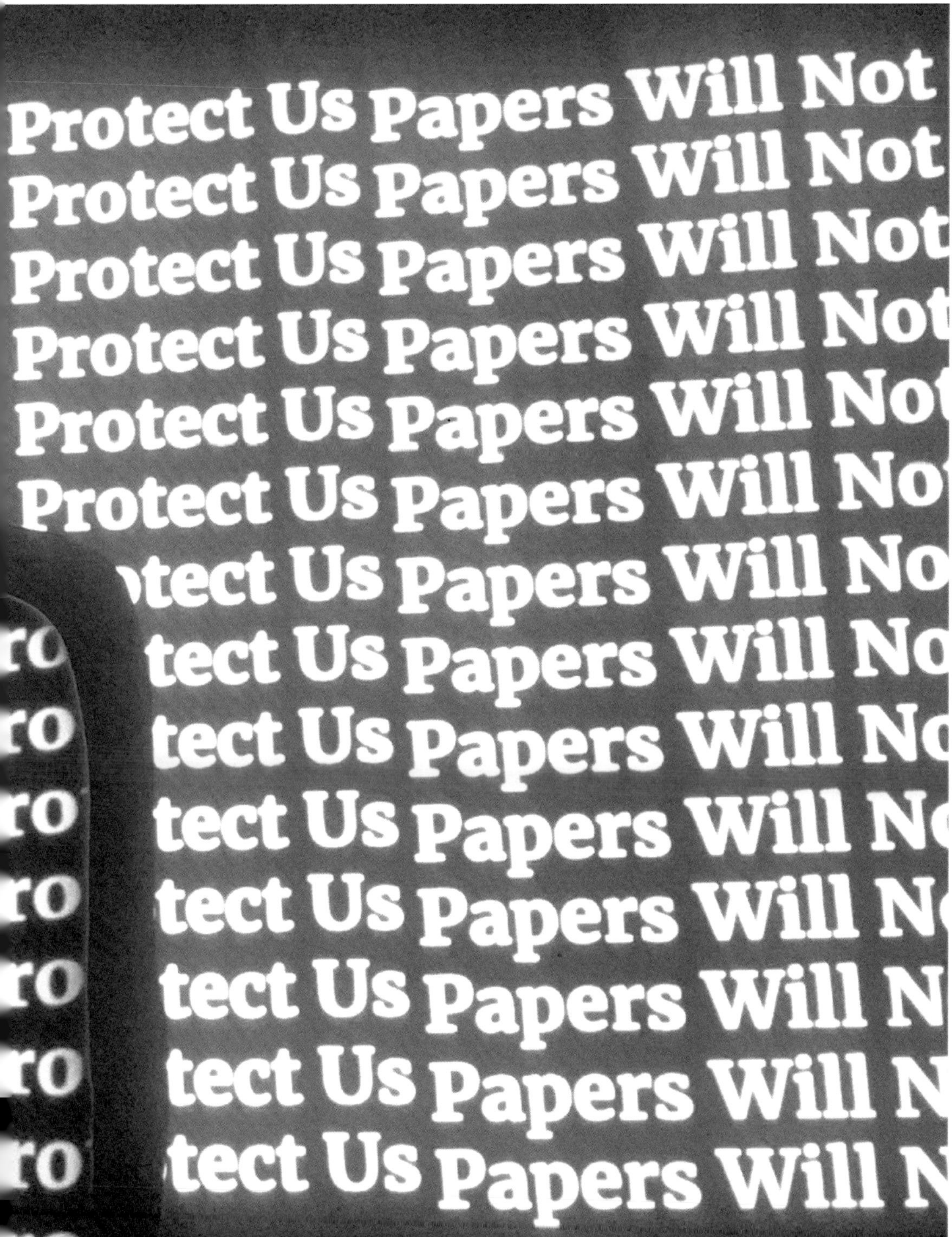

Protect Us Papers Will Not
Protect Us Papers Will Not
Protect Us Papers Will Not
Protect Us Papers Will Not
Protect Us Papers Will Not
Protect Us Papers Will No
tect Us Papers Will No
tect Us Papers Will No
tect Us Papers Will N
tect Us Papers Will N
tect Us Papers Will N
tect Us Papers Will N
tect Us Papers Will N
tect Us Papers Will N

I AM MORE THAN POLICY

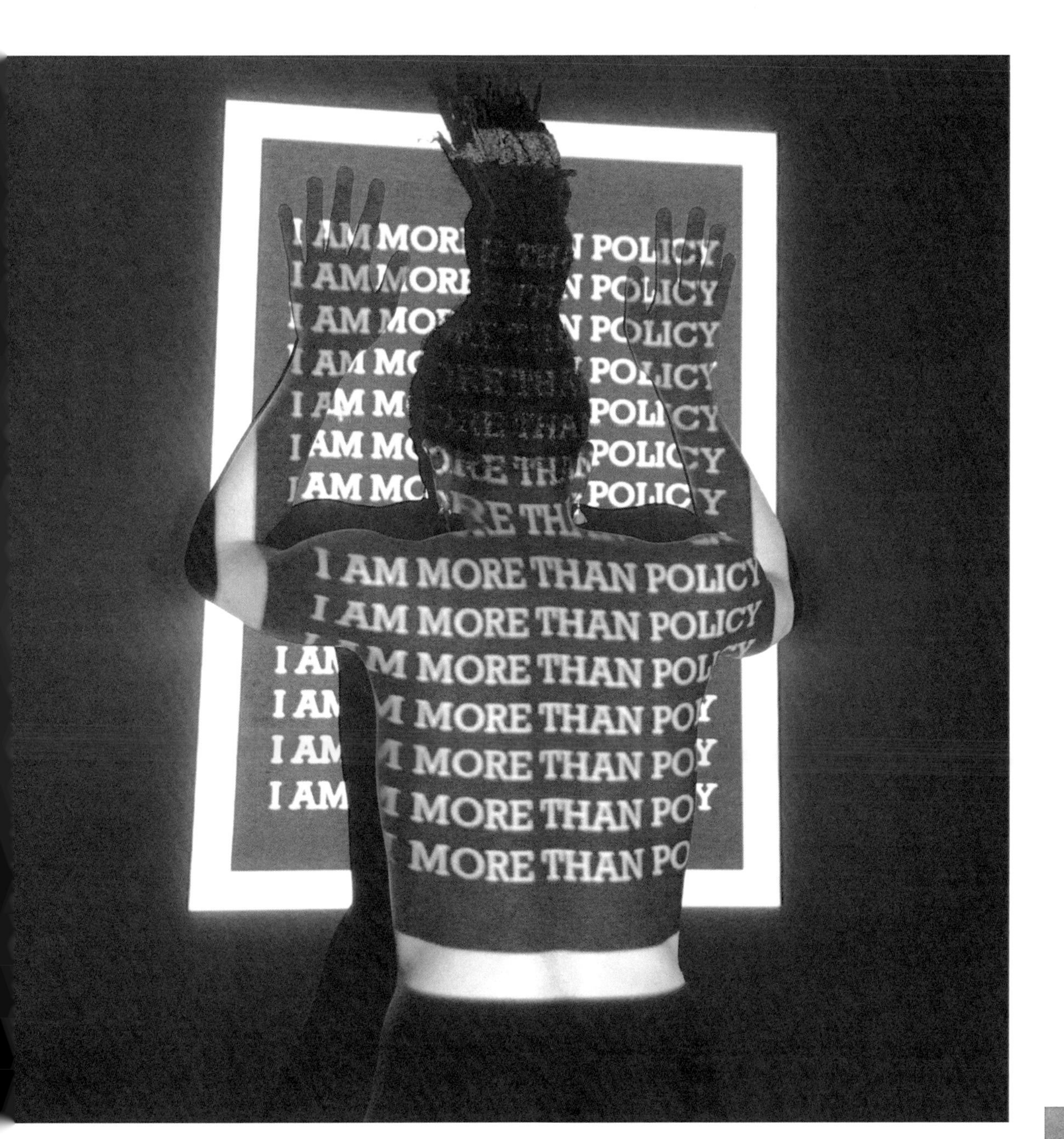
I AM MORE THAN POLICY
I AM MORE THAN POLICY

I AM MORE THAN POLIC
I AM MORE THAN POLICY
I AM MORE THAN POLICY
I AM MORE THAN POLICY
AM MORE THAN POLICY
AM MORE THAN
AM MORE THAN
AM MORE THAN
AM MORE THAN
AM MORE THAN
I AM MORE THAN
I AM MORE THAN
I AM MORE THAN
I AM MORE THAN

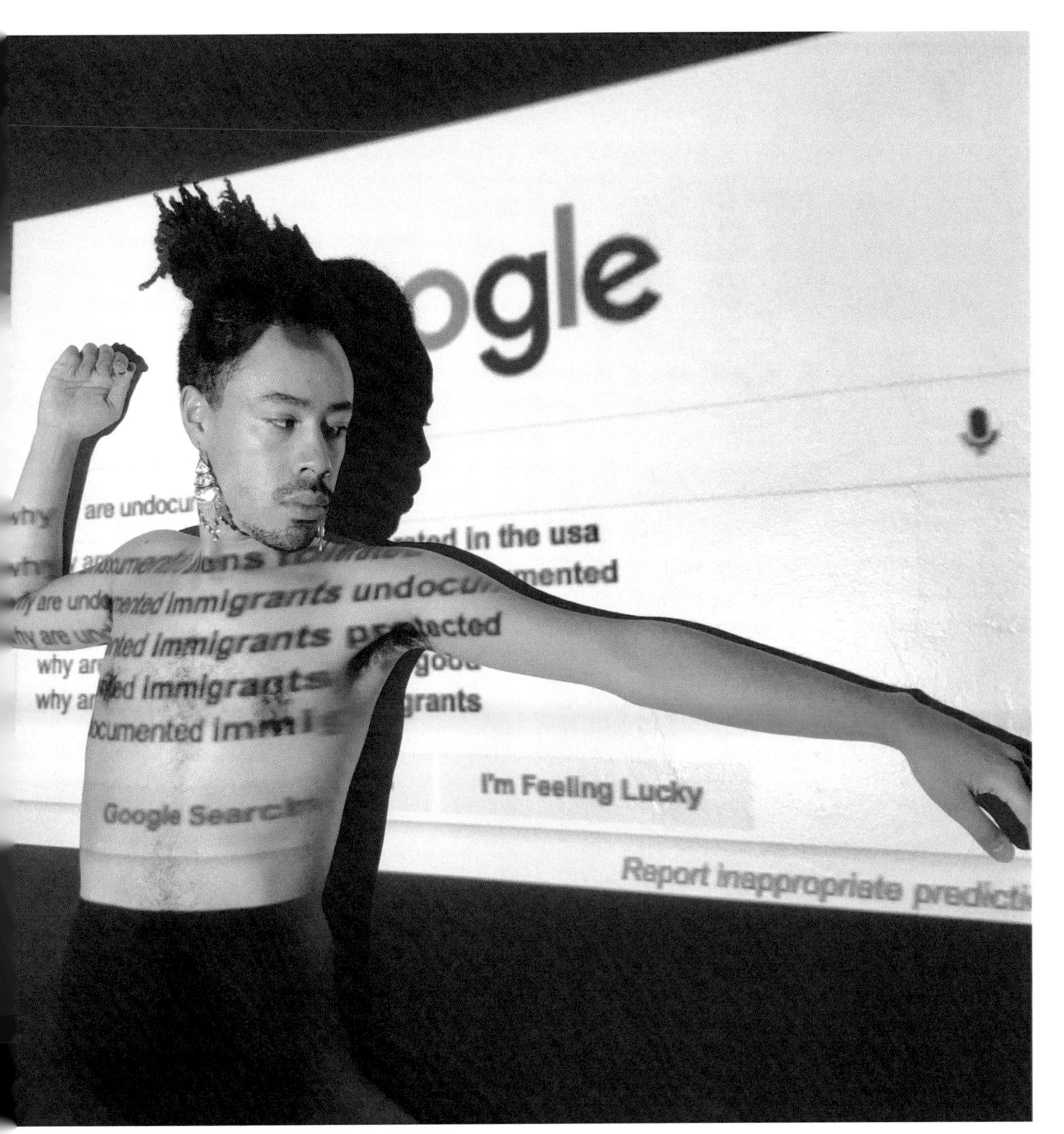
ogle
are undocu
in the usa
mented
immigrants undocu
immigrants protected
grants
I'm Feeling Lucky
Google Search
Report inappropriate predicti

Google
immigrants undocumented
ed immigrants
Search
I'm Feeling Lucky
Report inappropriate predic

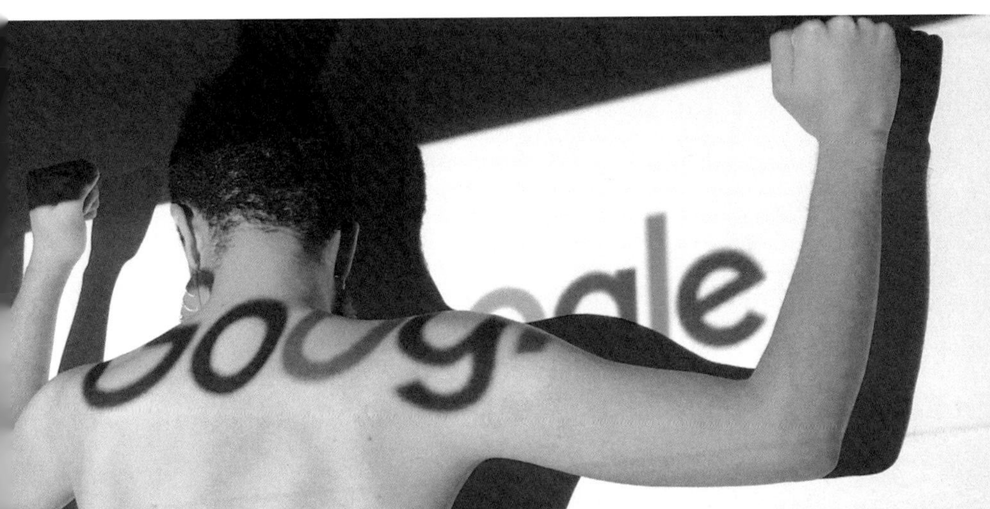
in the usa
documented
I'm Feeling Lucky
Report inappropriate predicti

MAMA'S BABY, PAPA'S MAYBE: INTERVIEW WITH AN ILLEGAL NEGRO

April, 2014

today, I am asked to answer questions about my ghost father, my negro flesh and the village I grew up in on the southern Pacific coast of Oaxaca, México. my soon-to-be lawyer does not notice how each of her questions attain a tighter grip of my neck. to distract the pain of a too-tight noose, I bite the tip of my thumb until my teeth go through my skin, red blood dripping onto my shirt, atop my heart— the blood rushes to my head, circles around *and around,* too much survival in my thoughts, too much fight-or-flight:

before i step out to use the bathroom, she tells me that I might get a green card, she can even set up a court hearing in as soon as eight days. but before, I have to finish telling my story over and over again for papers. not *my* story though. she wants *my mother's* story. my soon-to-be-lawyer likes my mother's story. it's more tragic. the tragedy assures that I won't just be another piece of Black flesh at the hearing————I'll be Black flesh with an excess of trauma (you know, the state loves a docile negro family).

after returning from the bathroom and answering every question, expanding into further detail every time I see my soon-to-be-lawyer slightly smile (she likes that I don't know his full name, though I have his last name), my soon-to-be-lawyer tells me, "I may not be able to help you," and has her first-year- law-student intern hand me a MetroCard to make sure I get home safe (all it takes is $2.75

to be kicked out of the office and on my way to the detention center /or prison / or detention and then prison / or detention and then prison and then deported).

shaking, my knees approximate the elevator, "G" pushes my scarecrow-like index finger. sixteen, fifteen, fourteen, I keep going down. when the doors open, I can't see the path. all I can see is blackness followed by a prolonged whiteness— I grab on to the right wall and get out. outside, I can feel my stomach getting ready to puke the three cups of 7-eleven's light-roast coffee I swallowed to get through my meeting. my eyes begin to roll to the back of my head (I can't afford to faint). I am lost ————my vision blurs.

somehow, I end up sitting on the staircase of a whitewashed wall st. entrance, I curl up, with my knees to my chest——my tears littering the asphalts of this island.

(I am tired of fugitive living)

today, I wanna to go to my mother's place: I wanna roll out the sheets and sleep on the floor. I don't care if I wake up with my nose stuffy, chest sore, feet cold——at least we'll be going through this together. and then I realize: my mother and I have always been going through *this* together and I've asked her to hold me so often that I have neglected to hold her too. today, I wanna practice a new kind of holding, a new type of fugitivity.

IMMIGRATION'S MANDATED DOCTOR VISIT

I arrived with sixteen dollars
and twenty-two cents,
a MetroCard
a dry mouth,
and a crying stomach,
but I lied anyways:

yes, I had a full breakfast.

***

When the White doctor called me
to his office,

he said:

just a physical.

***

Are you a sex worker? *No.*
Have you ever had sex for money? *No.*
Do you have any diseases? *No.*
But you're from Mexico. *It's México.*
Any health problems? *No.*
Can you lie down? *Uh-Yah.*
Pull down your pants just a little.

(I think I saw disgust in his eyes
as his hands colonized my uncut penis.

At some point, the room went black
and I almost screamed, brought back to
days of a b u s e & h u n g e r & p a i n.

He dismissed me from his office
not fast enough to control the PTSD though.)

***

Are you okay? *Of course.*
Not afraid of needles, right? *No.*
Have you eaten? *Yes.*
Great, we'll take some blood.

S u r e

***

I was let go seven test tubes of blood later,
made it outside, walked down half a block,
ordered a falafel sandwich from a halal truck
and fainted, or fell, or died,
or all three at the same time.

***

f u c k ***f u c k***

f u c k ***f u c k***

Spent $4 at the halal truck,
two dollars and seventy-eight cents
short for the Mega Bus now;

(that's why I didn't have breakfast)

F U C K.

***

I had nowhere to go, but at least

I had an ID to my name:
proof of personhood
(if one can call it *that*).

***

(Maybe a cute guy will come talk to me at
a bar & I can rail him into buying me
a drink and then steal the tip for the bus
—I hope it's cash tip—
or maybe I'll pretend I lost my card
and ask him for cash...)

F u c k,

I hate

men.

***

after the doctor's on West 14th // I found myself sitting on the dirt floor with my arms around

my knees // it was Wednesday night about to wed Thursday and my body

was still sitting there,

off of the NYC highway // my arms thought the needle was still

attached—doctor still taking blood.

for the first time, I wanted to believe

that this would soon be over// but then I realized // even if I got papers

I would still be a nigga & an NDN // I would still be a fag.

before the Megabus arrived, I walked to the public phone //I didn't mean to make a call,

I meant to find change.// I wondered: // *if I caress the coin*

slot enough, would nickels, dimes & quarters come out? // is this how a life is saved?

& that's when I realized:// *fuck, I am an alien*

I am an alien // I am an Alien // I am an ALIEN and

there is no need to wonder an'more becuz // we been changing the world—

we have survived the unspoken; // we been travelling galaxy after galaxy:

got my first princess doll from a galaxy called the "happy meal;"

had my first wet dream in a galaxy my mamá architected in Waltham, Massachusetts;//

kissed the first boi ever in a galaxy somewhere

between the Regal Player's stage and the dressing room;//

travelled the galaxy

of intense pleasure,// bites,// cuddles

and pillow talk in Cambridge, Massachusetts;//

transported myself from the galaxies of// street protests to

sexy undocuqueer steamy nights to

White Country Club University// to NYC faggy femme Caribbean house parties

to Sephora lipstick isles// and Goodwill's 50% off orange tag dress hunts.

before the Megabus arrives, I walk to the public phone.// I don't mean to make a call:

I mean to find change// and that's when I realize

that aliens cannot be tamed because we've been able to craft unimaginable lives.

before the Megabus arrives, I find the change I need when I

catch my reflection on the metal of the phone booth and remember the words of my mother:

escribe mi'jo, escribe.

***

I fell asleep at the bus station—

the Megabus driver let me pay $10 cash for the 4:55 ai-em bus.

***

I don't think I ate anything after the falafel,
but I got home and found safety in Diego's
Winnie-the-Pooh comforter hibernating in the linen closet.

—not sure how long I fell asleep for
but I'm sure glad Diego & Ashley have papers:
their story won't be easy, but at least we can
be each others' witness & extend our arms
when we are asked or don't know how to ask.

4. Are you afraid of being subjected to torture in your home country or any other country to which you may be returned?

☐ No ☒ Yes

If "Yes," explain why you are afraid and describe the nature of torture you fear, by whom, and why it would be inflicted.

the fear of torture is not particular to my country, it is particular to my body. i live in an ungovernable body. christina sharpe asks, "how does one memorialize the everyday" when living in a body like mine? do you get what i'm saying, sir?

i have already been subjected to torture, SIR. look at my medical records. look at my tuberculosis treatment. go find my sister's cadaver and look for the cause of death. read my poems, sir. read our poems, sir. poems are evidence, sir. this is the evidence, sir. READ POEMS.

Form I-589 (Rev. 05/16/17) N Page 6

is this enough

6. Have you or any member of your family included in the application ever committed any crime and/or been arrested, charged, convicted, or sentenced for any crimes in the United States?

☐ No ☒ Yes

If "Yes," for each instance, specify in your response: what occurred and the circumstances, dates, length of sentence received, location, the duration of the detention or imprisonment, reason(s) for the detention or conviction, any formal charges that were lodged against you or your relatives included in your application, and the reason(s) for release. Attach documents referring to these incidents, if they are available, or an explanation of why documents are not available.

i met a boy when i was nineteen / he had a scar below his left nipple./ when i asked him how he got it, / he covered it with his digits and said / "when i crossed." / that's when i told him i loved him. / loved him for crossing. / loved him for living. / loved him for sharing. / loved him for trusting. / loved him for reminding me we are human. / loved him for honesty. / loved him for stories. / loved him for poetry.

i met a boy when i was nineteen / he had spent two years, seventeen days in a detention center. / i swore to set the border on fire.

i met a boy when i was nineteen / & we did immoral things./ we are criminals, sir. / take me. take me. TAKE ME. TAKE ME. TAKEMETAKEME. TAAAAAAKE MEEE. TAKE ME. TAKE ME. TAKE ME. TAKE ME. ME

SIR?

The court document says that the state of New York
has found me to be abandoned by one, or both parents.

The court states that it is not in my best interest to
be removed from the United States, though they
will probably forget my name when my body is found
dead on a sidewalk, another Black faggot shot down.

Thank you for the protection New York,
I'll smile harder next time I see the NYPD
approaching me outside the subway station.

El documento judicial dice que el estado de Nueva York
me ha encontrado abandonado por uno, o por ambos padres.

El tribunal declara que no me conviene
ser retirado de los Estados Unidos, aunque
probablemente olvidará mi nombre cuando se encuentre mi cuerpo
muerto en una acera— otro joto Negro derribado.

Gracias por la protección Nueva York,
voy a sonreír más grande la próxima vez que vea a la policia
acercándose a mí fuera de la estación de metro.

I can no longer cross
// // / // borders.
My lungs, alma,
and mind,
can no longer swim,

So I have to // // / // hop;
// // / // // // / // Saltar.

And play
hide // // / // and // // / // seek in

OCCUPIED NDN LAND.

illegal is to poet when the government demands/needs your silence &

illegal is to have survived (again + again) & still be running &

illegal is to find pleasure on the lips of another alien & call it living

Department of Homeland Security
U.S. Citizenship and Immigration Services

I-797, Notice of Action

THE UNITED STATES OF AMERICA

RECEIPT NUMBER		CASE TYPE I485 APPLICATION TO REGISTER PERMANENT RESIDENCE OR ADJUST STATUS
RECEIPT DATE May 17, 2014	PRIORITY DATE May 1, 2014	APPLICANT PELAEZ LOPEZ, ALAN C.
NOTICE DATE October 8, 2014	PAGE 1 of 1	

ALAN CARLOS PELAEZ LOPEZ
NEW YORK NY 10038

Notice Type: Welcome Notice
Section: Other basis for adjustment

how does the former illegal alien recuperate years of living as a fugitive of the law? how does the former illegal alien make amends for the years of no contact with their family? how does the former illegal alien learn to live without hiding the minute an unaccounted knock on the door is heard? how does the former illegal alien begin to reclaim time and space as their own? how does the former illegal alien forget years and year and years of perpetual non-existence? how does the former illegal alien not internalize their criminalization? how does the former illegal alien go out into the world and remember that their body is no longer "illegal." how does the former illegal alien talk about their experience of knowing illegality more than they know legality? how does the former illegal alien pursue intimate relationships and just shrug off the years of no intimacy because they feared deportation? how does the former illegal alien learn to mourn in a manner that doesn't re-traumatize? how does the former illegal alien learn to love in a way that it is not informed from fear? how does the former illegal alien advocate for themselves at work, at school, at the public state house, at the laundry, at the supermarket, and at the bathhouse with their newly found "legality"?

Please see the additional information on the back. You will be notified separately about any other cases you filed.
NATIONAL BENEFITS CENTER
USCIS, DHS
P.O. BOX #648004
LEE'S SUMMIT MO 64064
Customer Service Telephone: (800) 375-5283

Form I-797 (Rev. 01/31/05) N

moments when i forget i am no longer "illegal":

i. outside detention centers
ii. at the sight of a white mini van
iii. when on hold with the free clinic
iv. right before accepting calls from prison
v. when i hear an unexpected knock on the door
vi. when TSA agents stick their fingers through my locs
vii. every time i am selected for special inspection[8] at the airport
viii. when asked for an ID & all i have is a scanned copy of my mexican passport
ix. when lovers ask me about the past and i unintentionally speak in the present tense

& the list continues but that shouldn't matter. what matters is that *this* should have never happened, but it did, and it continues to happen.

i didn't just live as an "illegal alien" in what is now know as the "united states." i lived as an "illegal alien" who is also the descendant of colonized north american ndns & people who arrived to the shores of the americas and auctioned off to the highest bidder. once auctioned and "owned," my ancestors moved through this continent as communal and::or private property.

8

(To: Immigrant; BCC: Citizen)

NOTICE OF INSPECTION

To protect your fellow passengers, the Transportation Security Administration (TSA) is required by law to inspect

You

During the inspection, you

may

break

TSA is

not liable for damages to you resulting from this necessary security precaution.

We appreciate your cooperation.

SECURITY

(To: Citizen)

INSPECTION

your fellow passenger

is

required by law to

break

for damages resulting from this necessary security precaution.

We appreciate you

SECURITY

let's do some historical arythmetic to get all this shit together:

$$\text{settler-colonialism} = \left(\frac{\text{settlement + slavery}^{2}}{\text{elimination - memory}} \right) \left(\text{criminalization of the “other”} \right)$$

and yet, we resist(ed) in quotidian ways because we knew::know that we are more than *papers* and that *this* (whatever it may be other than arythmetic) has a temporal end that we are always already fragmenting and approaching. *this* receives its injuries when we hold the hands of our loved ones in public. *this* receives its injuries when we remember the taste of iguana stew and roasted grasshoppers resting on clay bowls. *this* receives its injuries when we refuse to forget our roots::routes. *this* receives its injuries when we dare to accept and give love. *this* receives its injuries when we fail and try again. *this* receives its injuries at the moment of engaging in creation. *this* receives its injuries when we choose to recognize one another instead of waiting for the law to recognize us.

to survive fugitivity is to experiment with everyday forms of escape. to survive fugitivity is to hold joy, grief, anger, and pleasure all within the same hour. it's not romantic. escape(/ing) tends to hurt, and more often than not, escape(/ing) is unrecognizable. to survive fugitivity is to lean on that which punctures the body, fragmenting the idea that the body is ours, which is to say, to survive fugitivity is to experiment with the (re)making, (re)shaping, and (re) imagining of our bodies each day. ain't that intergalactic?

A FUTURE, ELSEWHERE

The first poem I ever wrote was in Spanish, I was in the 3rd grade. my mother came to hear me recite the piece. When I finished, all the mothers stared at me in confusion. See, the poem was about my desire to be a Seahorse because I wanted to give birth. Although my mother was concerned that her "son" wanted to be pregnant, she encouraged my poetry. I believe that the poem offered my mother parental relief: despite crossing a border, my mind was still able to imagine a future outside of our material reality. My mother was my first poetry teacher and for that, I am greatful. Her gift to me was an excess of vision. My mother's vision for our survival was to cross the border, so we did.

My mother's vision for life was marked as "illegal." In other words, those who have an excess of vision are punished by the law. I think this happens because our visions interrupt settler-futures. This reasoning has given me hope. The more of us that lean into our illegality, the more we envision. Some may call this a hallucination or tragic hope. I call this poetry. I call this a future. I call this an elsewhere, one that is shaped by all those who this empire tried to undo.

because poetry is how we reterritorialize

AN ARTIST MANIFESTO
FOR BLACK &/OR INDIGENOUS FOLK SURVIVING
EMPIRE

I believe in the Ghanaian concept of *Sankofa*: we must always go back and get that which we have lost. What we have lost as African-diasporic people, as Indigenous people, as queer people, as trans people, and as undocumented people is memory.

We have lost our memory.

Slavery, Indigenous genocide, homophobia, transphobia, xenophobia, anti-Blackness, patriarchy among hundreds of oppressive structures all have one thing in common: they work to uphold capitalism and White supremacy by making marginalized people forget who they are.

And just for one second, let me tell you who we are:

we are resilient,
messy,
powerful,
politically incorrect,
vulnerable,
loveable
and fierce as fuck individuals.

As marginalized people, we have been tasked with the responsibility to remember: remember that this was never the way *life* was supposed to be; remember that even if we cannot locate *home*, we can always imagine and craft such a place; remember that we are not alone & that our ancestors have left us blueprints of how to resist, survive and thrive, and those blueprints lay in the power of art.

In order to win the revolution, we are going to need artists:

One.
We Need Dancers,
DJs
and Singers

Resistance must no longer look like survival. We must live in order to resist. Dancers, DJ's and singers will be critical for the revolution. The beat of the drum, as our indigenous ancestors have taught us, is the beat of our heart. We will need DJ's to remix our drum beats when we feel that we are alone in the world. When we think we can no longer resist, we will need dancers to show us how to regain the movement and power of our imaginations. We will need singers who vocalize our truths in music so that we do not forget where we come from. We will need dancers, dj's and singers for the revolution.

Two.
We Need Porn Stars, Strippers and Pole Dancers

Pleasure, intimacy and the erotics must be part of our revolution, so we are going to need the art and guidance of porn stars, strippers and pole dancers. In this society, Black people, queer people, trans people, mentally ill people, immigrants, youth, poor people and incarcerated people are typically viewed as perverted and savage. We will need porn stars, strippers and pole dancers to re-appropriate the meaning of perversion and pleasure. Kinship is the most pleasurable, intimate and erotic human interaction in my world. We will need porn stars, strippers and pole dancers to teach us how to be comfortable with pleasure, intimacy and the erotics because I am not sure if I can fight in a revolution that doesn't allow me to build queer and trans kinship that will propel us into the future.

Three.
We Need Writers and Painters

If we are going to survive this era, we are going to need to pay close attention to writers and painters. I mean writers like Staceyann Chin who doesn't give a fuck about respectability politics. Chin will be unapologetic about her hella melanated lesbian Black ass, and tell us about the first time she used a tampon and ripped out all her hairs. And we are going to need damn skilled painters like Alexa Bow who will paint her undocumented trans sisters into existence when this system has fooled itself into believing that it has disposed of us. We are going to need writers and painters who can document our past, our present and our future.

Four.
We Need Healers and Farmers

I'm sure I can get you all on board with this one: we need healers and farmers now more than ever because capitalism works best when we forget how to support for ourselves. I'd like to quote my trans Afro-Mexican sibling, Leo Orleans, since he always reminds me that if I don't learn how to farm, I will not be ready for the apocalypse. We need farmers who can teach us how to bring life into this world, when as marginalized people, it seems that our lives are taken away more than they are celebrated. But, we cannot do this without healers. We are going to need brujas, curanderas and santeras who will teach us how to survive. We are going to have to learn how to take care for one another because the reality is that healers need healing too, and we can't just take, take and take, because that's the number one foundation of capitalism. So, remember, we are going to need healers and farmers for the revolution.

Five.
We Need Cholas and Gangsters

We will need the very particular skills that only Cholas and Gangsters can teach us: hustling, love, and reconciliation. We are going to need Gangsters who can teach us how to protect and love our hoods and one another. We are going to need Cholas from East LA, Chicago, and the Bronx to teach us the real meaning of resilience, sisterhood, having each other's back, and how to have popping eyebrows while fighting the system. We have under appreciated the strength, the brilliance and the excellence of Cholas and Gangsters, and it is not too late to turn to them for leadership and guidance.

Six.
We Need Photographers, Cartoonists and Illustrators

Photography is one of the most dangerous technological inventions, as it was primarily used to dehumanize Indigenous people, and later, to surveille the Black body. We need photographers, cartoonists and illustrators to counter-surveille. We need to document intimate moments of resilience, because the revolution is about the small changes in our lives. We are going to need photographers who divest from representations of "good citizenship" and invest in chaos, mess and disobedience. We are going to need cartoonists who can teach us that in our hardest times, we are still embodied and animated subjects with the possibility of love, pain, joy, orgasms, and everything in between. We are going to need illustrators who teach us how to see ourselves when we think that all that there is is darkness.

The revolution will be led by artists, and if it is not, it is not a revolution that will change culture, society, or politics.

I love you lots):

I really hope we are

I don't wanna normalize any of it

And I think I am starting to

i think we are all collectively exhausted

Sometimes, I think everything that's happening is a dream we will wake up from

I love you too

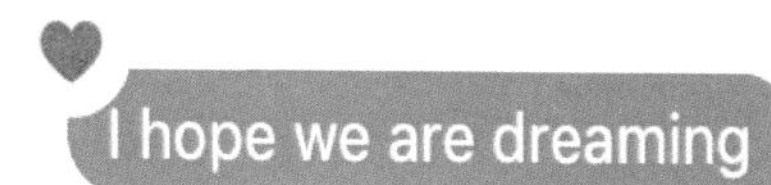

We can't accept this reality

We have to refuse as hard as we can

But we need to hold each other to refuse

I want to learn to love better, to hold tighter

UNKNOWN

Page 6
Title: *Fragments of Mixtec and Zapotec Territories*
digital drawing
Note: This map is informed by a map I found ripped in half on the side of the road in Pinotepa Nacional, Oaxaca, MX.

Pages 10 and 11
Title: *Genealogies*
mixed media: hand cut collage and digital drawing
Note: The photograph of the child is one of the only two childhood photographs I had growing up. In this photograph, I am four and a student at an elementary school in Mexico City. For a holiday celebration, all students were to perform a musical number and dressed up according to the genre of the music and the region from where the music originated. I was one of the few children asked to dress as an "Indian" because of my Oaxacan roots (I did not have the words back then to be specific and identify my Zapotec community). I find this image fascinating as the attire isn't linked to any specific Indigenous community in Mexico, but instead, represents the colonial fantasy of the "Mexican Indian," which is perpetuated by non-Indigenous Mexicans and Eurodescendants living in Mexico.

Page 13
Title: *Language, I do not speak. I scream.*
digital poster
Note: In 2017, I offered a downloadable link of this poster for people to print and use at their own discretion.

UNDOCUMENTED

Page 20
Title: *Warning*
photograph
Note: This photograph was taken in the summer of 2014 at Friendship Park / El Parque de la Amistad, which is a half-acre park that rests on two countries: the U.S. and Mexico. There are two border fences in the middle of the park. When I visited, I was still undocumented and was only able to take two photographs before a border patrol car turned on the alarm, drove to me, and asked me to step away from the fence.

HYPER-DOCUMENTATION

Page 47
Title: *Altar/Alter (1 of 40)*
installation

9/05/2017 – 9/10/2017
Fruitvale, Oakland, CA
Note: On September 5, 2017, President Donald Trump announced his plan to phase out DACA, which would affect approximately 690,000 – 800,000 undocumented people in the United States. This altar/alter was produced in response to the announcement.

Page 50
Title: *AlieN InvasioN*
digital collage

Page 52
Title: *Fugitive Subject*
hand cut collage

Page 54
Title: *Criminal Subject*
hand cut collage

Page 56
Title: *Fugitive Subject 2*
hand cut collage

Page 58
Title: *Criminal Subject 2*
hand cut collage

Pages 60-61
Title: *Legalize Aliens*
digital erasure poems

Page 64
Title: *Google Maps Directs Me Home*
digital collage
Note: The photograph that provides the background to this collage was also taken in the summer of 2014 at Friendship Park / El Parque de la Amistad, which is a half-acre park that rests on two countries: the U.S. and Mexico. There are two border fences in the middle of the park. When I visited, I was still undocumented and was only able to take two photographs before a border patrol car turned on the alarm, drove to me, and asked me to step away from the fence.

Pages 66-67
Title: *Papers Will Not Protect Us (series)*
digital images

Pages 70-72
Title: *I Am More Than Policy (series)*
digital images

Pages 73-74
Title: *are undocumented [ ]* (series)
digital images

Page 75
Title: *why are [ ]*
digital image

Page 88
Title: *Fugitive Affect: a self-portrait*
photograph
Note: Between 2015- 2018, I began photographing my shadow whenever I experienced moments of either fight/flight and/or gender dysphoria. The shadow is also representative of the shadow- standpoint that undocumented immigrants are forced to inhabit by virtues of a U.S. legal system that deems them "illegal aliens," and thus, always already suspect.

POST DOCUMENTS

Page 91
Title: *1-797 Notice of Action*
digital document
Note: Red overlapping text reads: "how does the former illegal alien recuperate years of living as a fugitive of the law? how does the former illegal alien make amends for the years of no contact with their family? how does the former illegal alien learn to live without hiding the minute an unaccounted knock on the door is heard? how does the former illegal alien begin to reclaim time and space as their own? how does the former illegal alien forget years and years and years of perpetual non-existence? how does the former illegal alien not internalize their criminalization?how does the former illegal alien go out into the world and remember that their body is no longer "illegal." how does the former illegal talk about their experience of knowing illegality more than they know legality? how does the former illegal pursue intimate relationships and just shrug off the years of no intimacy because they feared deportation? how does the former illegal learn to mourn in a manner that doesn't re-traumatize? how does the former illegal alien learn to love in a way that is not informed from fear? how does the former illegal alien advocate for themselves at work, at school, at the public stat house, at the laundry, at the supermarket, and at the bathhouse with their newly found 'legality'?."

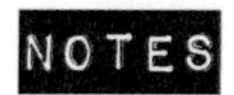

NOTES

UNKNOWN

Pages 10-11: These pieces are after Danez Smith's poem "Untitled and About Sadness" (2014).

UNDOCUMENTED

Black NDN Crosses Border at 5-Years-Old (Zapotec): This poem is not in legible Zapotec. The words that appear are pieced together from UC Santa Cruz's "Zapotec Language Project." In 2017, I returned to Oaxaca for the first time in 18 years and after much interrogation of every family member I could find, I came to learn that there was hesitation (and perhaps shame) in naming the fact that we are not far removed from family members who spoke Zapotec. In response to this hesitation, I began yearning for language. I unknowingly wrote this poem after looking through UCSC's online dictionary and when I presented it to Zapotec-speakers, they looked at me in confusion and later taught me how to render this poem in Isthmust Zapotec and Sierra Norte Zapotec. This iteration of the poem lives in its original form as a reminder of the first moment I critically thought about grappling with my ancestral language.

"'sick' in america": This poem triangulates the fugitivity of runaway slaves under the Fugitive Slave Act of 1850, an Indigenous fugitivity produced by the sequestration of Indigenous children during the late 19 th century to the early 20 th century (the allotment and assimilation era), and the fugitivity of the "illegal alien" produced by the Johnson-Reed Act / Immigration Act of 1924. The quote that appears on footnote seven is taken from Tavia Nyongo's essay, "Habeas ficta : fictive ethnicity, affecting representations, and slaves on screen," which first appeared in the edited volume *Migrating the Black Body: The African Diaspora and Visual Culture* (2017).

HYPER-DOCUMENTATION

"Found Poem": all words in this piece are taken from AP News' story "9 die in immigrant-smuggling attempt in sweltering truck" (July 23, 2017).

Page 56: This poem borrows from the theoretical frameworks of Deborah Miranda's *Bad Indians: a tribal memoir* (2012) and Joy DeGruy's *Post Traumatic Slave Syndrome: America's Legacy of Enduring Injury and Healing* (2005).

"Mama's Baby, Papa's Maybe: Interview with an Illegal Negro": This poem borrows from and is in conversation with Hortense J. Spillers' article "Mama's Baby, Papa's Maybe: An American Grammar Book" (1987).

Page 72: This poem borrows from the theoretical frameworks of Christa E. Sharpe's *In the Wake : On Blackness and Being* (2016).

Page 98: This poem makes reference to Gilles Deleuze and Felix Guattari's "Rhizome Versus Tree."

Madre, este libro es para ti, para nosotrxs, y para nuestro pueblo.

Jaselia Gratini, Laura Marcela Gonzalez, and Andres del Castillo: thank you for the necessary cultural work you led in Massachusetts with immigrant creatives. "MigrArte" changed me deeply.

All the flowers & chocolates to Sonia Guiñansaca and Kemi Bello who created the first digital archive of undocumented artists.

A shout out to my UndocuWriting cohort: Alex Aldana, Stephanie (Soultree) Camba, Marco Antonio Flores, Alexa Bow, May Liang, Yunuen Rodriguez, Yahaira Carrillo, Alexandra Samarron, Razeen Zaman, Emilia Fiallo, Eunice Alejandra (& again) Kemi Bello and Sonia Guiñansaca.

Thank you to the friends who witnessed and held me in CT and NY between 2012-2015, the years that shaped this book: Heather Mooney, Carina Nieto, Crystal Rodriguez, Adavia Thornton, Marisol del Monte, Aileen Medina, Jocelyn Collen, Molly Camp, Kristen Seeto, Durell Snow, Johanna Garvey, Eileen Harris, Rachel Lang, Brianna Perkins, & Danilo Machado.

Again, Jaselia Gratini: thank you for calling when I couldn't call. Thank you for your love. Thank you for reading & re-reading & calling each time.

Ra Malika Imhotep: giiiirl, we still alive & creating. I am honored for the mutual witnessing we have for one another. Here is to more collaboration, more phone calls, & Blacker visions.

Jennif(f)er Tamayo: you were the first person to ask, "where's the book, mami?." Thank you for believing, encouraging, and always keeping it 100.

Breena Nuñez and Lawrence Lindell: thank you for opening up your home for countless sessions of coffee, cartoons, and venting while we each worked on our manuscripts.

Caleb Luna: thank you for your commitment to art, friendship, and risk(s).

My Bay Area chosen family— I love you: Ola Osaze, Eniola Abioye, Lorn Kategaya, Wahira LaBelle, Eri Oura Kyoko, Robbie Pages, Brecklyn Walters, Valeria Suarez, Sandra Ramirez, Leo Orleans, China Ruiz, Yujane Chen, & many more.

To the artists, thinkers, and agitators who generously invited me to explore new galaxies: Monique Nguyen, Lily Huang, Beth Piatote, Leigh Raiford, C.S. Giscombe, Elmaz Abinader, Kris Sealey, Carol Ann Davis, Vanessa Rochelle Lewis, (again) Johanna Garvey, & so many more.

Thank you to my family that is the Black LGBTQIA+ Migrant Project. Blessed we be, always.

Thank you to the editors at the following outlets who published poems from this manuscript, sometimes in earlier forms: *Survivance: Indigenous Poesis Vol IV., Pittsburgh Poetry Review, Red Ink: International Journal of Indigenous Literature, Arts, & Humanities, Vinyl, Gemstone Readings, A Quiet Courage, & bozalta.*

FUGITIVITY, SEQUESTRATION, AND ESCAPE: TACTICS IN THE REALM OF LANGUAGE

A CONVERSATION WITH ALAN PELAEZ LOPEZ

Greetings! Thank you for talking to us about your process today! Can you introduce yourself, in a way that feels the most, well, you?

For sure! My name is Alan, and I'm a thinker, writer, lover, and an introvert with a capricorn rising, scorpio moon, and taurus sun. I was born in Mexico City, but both my parents are from Oaxaca, MX, and while I lived in MX, I regularly migrated between Oaxaca and Mexico City. When I left the country, I migrated to East Boston, MA, so I guess I can say that East Boston was the first home I had in the states, but there's something about the states that don't quite feel like home, so I tend to joke and say that I live on the internet.

How did you come to see yourself as a creative?

I started making jewelry at the age of six to sell at bus stops and laundromats, so that was my first creative practice. At first, I was using acrylic beads wherever I could find them in the three-block radius of the apartment my mother and I rented in East Boston. As the years went by, the world of materials opened up and I began exploring wood, mixed-metals, leather, and copper. Because I was a child jeweler, most folks around me saw an artist and encouraged my art. At one point, I used to tell my mom that I was going to be a textile designer and would spend hours filling out 8.5' x 11' sheets of paper with elaborate designs. I had so many sheets of paper that I started writing bad rhyme poems on them, and you know, I hung on to the bad poems and now I'm here, a dique "poeta."

What's a "poet" anyway?

Hmm, ain't that a question! I believe that every community has poets and that poetry lives in pattern-making, map-making, weaving, songs, gossip, and in any form of storytelling. Poetry, for me, has little to do with pen and paper. In my personal life, poetry has been an articulation (a rendering) that one person offers to the world without the expectation of a receiver, or a witness. So, in this case, poetry is an organic action that one's body produces. I don't believe in "training," for if one needs training to offer without expectation, then what does that say about how we relate to people?

As a poet who is also Indigenous, Black, queer, and gender non-conforming, my role is to attempt to grapple with experiences and sentiments that I don't know how to describe to others, but desperately want to communicate. For example, my work ventures into multimedia because the singular letter has never been enough. I move in a body that experiences the world through sound, images, color, smell, and taste, so a lot of my poetry centers those affective registers as opposed to the letter. Living at the intersection of these targeted and marginalized identities makes me a poet who doubles both as a creative and cultural organizer. I hope that my work can shift culture, but that's not why I create. I create so that I can better understand the world that is alive around me, as opposed to assuming I know what and who is alive around me.

Can you say more about cultural organizing? What do you see as your cultural and social role in the literary / artistic / creative community and beyond?

I entered the immigrant rights movement ten years ago, and got sucked into the world of community organizing fairly quickly. I'm proud to say that I was a solid community organizer, but I'm a stronger cultural worker. When community organizers want to respond to recently approved laws through policy briefings and lobbying, I respond with images, cultural commentary, and poems that are more digestible. In order to do this work, I have to study everything around me: I have to read the law, I have to go to the briefings, I consult lawyers, I talk with community members about how their life is changing or is expected to change with the latest legal shift, and then, I create. Although my art appears to be solitary, my art is community informed.

As a writer, I have to interact with the larger literary world, and those interactions are always changing and shifting. I don't have an MFA, and at first, I was insecure about lacking "knowledge," which was a sentiment that was produced at literature conferences. Often, the first question someone would ask me after my name, was/continues to be, "where did you earn your MFA?" Now, I immediately say: "I don't have one." Before, I use to explain why I didn't have one, which, to be honest, felt shitty. Yeah, that's a great word, shitty. I think that the literary world is moving away from the emphasis they have on MFA's, but I'm not sure what the shift means at this moment. As an experimental writer, I think that my social role is to be in dialogue with artists outside literature. I believe in deep collaboration and I hope that my work can add to the ecosystem of Indigenous and Black migrant artists.

Talk about the process or instinct to move these poems (or your work in general) as independent entities into a body of work. How and why did this happen? Have you had this intention for a while?

Most of the poems in this collection were first conceived between 2013 and 2015. At the time, I was still undocumented and traveling between Connecticut and New York City searching for a lawyer who could find an opening in my story that would allow me to initiate an immigration case that wouldn't trigger an immediate order of removal, followed by a ten-year ban from the country. For about a year, every lawyer I met expressed no possibility of adjustment. One day, I took a bus to Washington D.C. and a single visit changed everything, and thus, my journey for an adjustment of status perpetually had me on the road. To manage my anxiety on Amtrak, the NYC subway, and the Metro North Railway, I carried a legal notepad and wrote from the moment I sat down until I reached my destination. If I didn't write during my commutes, I would enter an internal spiral where I'd continually imagined a judge deny my application and deport me within the same day. So, the instinct that moved these poems was my need to protect myself from spiraling.

When you were writing in your legal pad, did you envision this collection as a collection or understand your process as writing? How or how not?

No, in my mind, I was writing because I was afraid that if I didn't, that I would lose hope and shut down. I do remember calling my friends Crystal, Jase, and Heather on several occasions. I would either ask them to meet me in person, or to listen to my poetry. Each time I wrote, I found out more about myself than I previously had not known, and I desperately needed someone to witness me and assure me that none of the violence I had gone through was acceptable.

Some of the poems on the legal pads made it onto word documents by coincidence: I was a bit of an emotional wreck when I was writing and often found myself crying onto the pad. In fear that I'd lose the writing, I would transfer the pieces from damp sheets of paper onto Word Documents. There were times that I felt the poems I had composed laid me bare naked, and because my moon is in Scorpio, I ripped the sheets out of the legal pad and threw them out.

So, no, I never intended to write a book. In fact, that's why this collection is so experimental.

Ah, will you say more about the experimentation of this collection?

When I first printed all the poetry pieces I had saved, I felt overwhelmed. There were poems about my mother, a few dozen poems written during and/or after direct actions I had been a part of over the years, and quite a few vignettes that didn't tell a narrative, but served as reminders of the thoughts that would enter my mind at all hours of the day.

During the selection process, I wanted to think through my own story in a way that honored my experience but didn't reveal too much information about my crossing as an unaccompanied minor or the lives of my family members.

When I put together the first iteration of the manuscript, I was angry; I was angry with lawyers who asked questions without following-up with me about how I was to take care of myself thereafter; I was angry at the fact that I didn't have the language to articulate to my friends and family what kind of support I needed; and I was angry at all the immigration forms I had to fill out on a day-to-day basis.

My anger needed an outlet, and betraying poetic form felt like a good outlet at the time. So, I took to visual art, writing in forms, and leaning on my PTSD to craft a methodological approach to render a story that wasn't invested in resolution, but invested in revelation. In all of this, I began to exercise my right to opacity.

I love that you're talking about a poet's right to opacity. Were there any teachers, friends, mentors, or authors that helped you think in this way?

Yes, Jaselia Gratini's friendship and poetic practice informs some of the epistemological approaches of my work. Jase is a Black poet from the Dominican Republic who (over the last ten years) has made me think critically about the practice of storytelling as a tool that can oppress or liberate. Through sharing poems on Facebook messenger, text, and sleep overs, Jase and I have interrogated the way in which U.S. public policy and immigration policy often demand stories of catastrophic violence from Black and migrant communities. Critical interrogations of storytelling with Jaselia have shaped my need to betray traditional storytelling practices of beginning, middle, climax, and end, in addition to betraying the way in which the Western world understands "poetry."

During the editing of this manuscript, I dived into a deep study of Theresa Hak Kyung Cha's *Dictee;* Jennif(f)er Tamayo's collection of poetry and art, *Red Missed Aches, Read Missed Aches, Red Mistakes, Read Mistakes*; Evie Shockley's poetry collection, *semiautomatic*; June Jordan's collection of essays, *Affirmative Acts*; Ntozake Shange's writings on cultural production, *lost in language & sound: or how i found my way to the arts*; Christina Sharpe's *In The Wake: On Blackness and Being;* and Edwidge Danticat's magnificent essay collection, *Create Dangerously: The Immigrant Artist at Work*. Although I don't personally know most of these writers, I consider the books they wrote my friends, and I'm so grateful for both the books and their author's.

Speaking of texts that helped you revise your collection, what does your title represent? How was it generated? Talk about the way you titled the book, and how your process of naming (individual pieces, sections, etc.) influences you.

The first part of the title, *Intergalactic Travels*, is taken from the title of a poem in the collection that traces six undocumented crossings, five are representative of personal friends, and one is representative of mine. Five of the six crossings described are of Black migrants from Latin America, the Caribbean, and West Africa. The second part of the title, poems from a fugitive alien, indirectly refer to the Fugitive Slave Acts of 1793 and 1850, in which the U.S. legal system marked the running away from a plantation an illegal act in which the enslaved person was to be hunted, returned, and disciplined by their owner. In combining the reality of a historical racialized fugitivity and a contemporary racialized and ethnicized fugitivity marked as "alien," the title of the book invites readers to question the ethical and moral implications of the U.S. legal system.

If you've noticed, the collection is broken down into five parts: "Unknown," "Undocumented," "Hyper-Documentation," "Post-Documents," and "A Future, Elsewhere," perspectively. Each section serves as its own world. The "Unknown" attempts to make sense of a history that I, as the author, know little of, but can't deny. In that section, I posit European colonialism in the Americas, the trans*Atlantic slave trade, and the formulation of the "illegal alien" together. In "Undocumented," I explore PTSD as both an inheritance and a reality that is alive in my body by virtue of my migration. "Hyper-Documentation" is the section that deals with my (unsuccessful) attempts to apply for a T-Visa, followed by political asylum, and finally, a peculiar case that I reveal little about. In, "Post-Documents," I attempt to think fugitivity, sequestration, and escape as governmental tactics that exist in the realm of language, and not necessarily in the realm of status. And finally, "A Future, Elsewhere," serves as an opening, a world of reflection, a world committed to offering a type of holding that breathes outside the hold of the slave ship, the hold of detainment, and the holding cell.

Each section is so deeply personal, why publish this book when you are not yet a U.S. citizen? Can you talk about the risk of being a formerly undocumented poet who can be deported from the U.S.?

I think about this often. This book is more than just a poetry collection, this book is my testimony. As someone who can still be removed from the U.S. at any moment, I can't assure that whoever is deporting me will actually hear my side of the story, so I have to write it into the archive. The U.S. is obsessed with paper traces, so I am engaging in what they're good at: the manipulation of words, images, and stories. My body may be deported, but this book will remain here to tell a story that didn't start with me crossing the border in 1999, but a story that started in the fifteenth century when a group of men-with-no-heart decided that Indigenous people in the continent of Africa were not human and thus kidnapped, transported, auctioned, and enslaved them in what is now known as "Mexico."

Even in the face of detainment and deportation, I write because I know I can. My body, my heart, my digits produced this object because the object was necessary.

What would be the best possible outcome for this book? What might it do in the world, and how will its presence as an object facilitate your creative role in your community and beyond?

The best possible outcome is for people to believe: believe that the shit that happened to me is true, and believe that the cause of this violence is (and continues to be) the law and those who are in positions to write and push it forward. I want this book to make people uncomfortable with their dependence in a legal system that from the start has been committed to maintaining the structure of settler-colonialism in the Americas.

I also want this book to be an object of possibility. I end the book with a text message because although the law dehumanizes us, we can humanize each other. I want other (un)documented and under-documented community members to know that we are more than status. We're people who happen to be undocumented, that's it. There's more to us. There is so much possibility, but that possibility hurts and I hope that we can explore that hurt in a way that allows us to be compassionate with and to ourselves.

ALAN PELAEZ LOPEZ is an AfroIndigenous poet, installation, and adornment artist from Oaxaca, México. They are the author of the art and poetry collection, *Intergalactic Travels: poems from a fugitive alien* (The Operating System, 2020), and the chapbook, *to love and mourn in the age of displacement* (Nomadic Press, 2020). Their poetry has been nominated for the Pushcart Prize and "Best of the Net," as well as published in *Best New Poets, Best American Experimental Writing, POETRY, Puerto Del Sol, Everyday Feminism*, & elsewhere. Pelaez Lopez has received fellowships and/or residencies from Submittable, the Museum of the African Diaspora, VONA/ Voices, and UC Berkeley. They live in Oakland, CA & the internet (as @MigrantScribble).

WHY PRINT / DOCUMENT?

*The Operating System uses the language "print document" to differentiate from the book-object as part of our mission to distinguish the act of documentation-in-book-FORM from the act of publishing as a backwards-facing replication of the book's agentive *role* as it may have appeared the last several centuries of its history. Ultimately, I approach the book as TECHNOLOGY: one of a variety of printed documents (in this case,* bound*) that humans have invented and in turn used to archive and disseminate ideas, beliefs, stories, and other evidence of production.*

Ownership and use of printing presses and access to (or restriction of printed materials) has long been a site of struggle, related in many ways to revolutionary activity and the fight for civil rights and free speech all over the world. While (in many countries) the contemporary quotidian landscape has indeed drastically shifted in its access to platforms for sharing information and in the widespread ability to "publish" digitally, even with extremely limited resources, the importance of publication on physical media has not diminished. In fact, this may be the most critical time in recent history for activist groups, artists, and others to insist upon learning, establishing, and encouraging personal and community documentation practices. Hear me out.

With The OS's print endeavors I wanted to open up a conversation about this: the ultimately radical, transgressive act of creating PRINT /DOCUMENTATION in the digital age. It's a question of the archive, and of history: who gets to tell the story, and what evidence of our life, our behaviors, our experiences are we leaving behind? We can know little to nothing about the future into which we're leaving an unprecedentedly digital document trail — but we can be assured that publications, government agencies, museums, schools, and other institutional powers that be will continue to leave BOTH a digital and print version of their production for the official record. Will we?

As a (rogue) anthropologist and long time academic, I can easily pull up many accounts about how lives, behaviors, experiences — how THE STORY of a time or place — was pieced together using the deep study of correspondence, notebooks, and other physical documents which are no longer the norm in many lives and practices. As we move our creative behaviors towards digital note taking, and even audio and video, what can we predict about future technology that is in any way assuring that our stories will be accurately told – or told at all? How will we leave these things for the record?

In these documents we say:
WE WERE HERE, WE EXISTED, WE HAVE A DIFFERENT STORY

- Elæ [Lynne DeSilva-Johnson], Founder/Creative Director
THE OPERATING SYSTEM, Brooklyn NY 2018

The Operating System has always understood itself as an explicitly *queer* project: not only insofar as that it was founded, consistently produces work by, and is staffed by primarily queer creative practitioners, but also in its commitment to *queering* the normative forms and expectation of that practice. If to queer something is to "take a look at its foundations and question them," troubling its limits, biases, and boundaries, seeking possibilities for evolution and transformation, then queering is written into the DNA of the Operating System's mission in every action and project, regardless of the orientation or gender of its maker.

However: while all the publications and projects we support encourage radical divergence and innovation, we are equally dedicated to recentering the canon through committing parts of our catalog to amplifying those most in danger of erasure. First, this took to the form of our translation and archival oriented *Glossarium: Unsilenced Texts* series, started in 2016, and in 2018 we made concrete our already active mission to work with creators challenging gender normativity with our *KIN(D)* Texts & Projects* series. Projects and publications under the *KIN(D)** moniker are those developed by creators who are transgender, nonbinary, genderqueer, androgynous, third gender, agender, intersex, bigender, hijra, two-spirit, and/or whose gender identity refuses a label.

Titles in this series include:

HOAX - Joey De Jesus
RoseSunWater - Angel Dominguez
Intergalactic Travels: poems from a Fugitive Alien - Alan Pelaez Lopez
A Bony Framework for the Tangible Universe - D. Allen
Opera on TV - James Lowell Brunton
Hall of Waters - Berry Grass
Transitional Object - Adrian Silbernagel
Sharing Plastic - Blake Neme
The Ways of the Monster - Jay Besemer
Marys of the Sea; #Survivor - Joanna C. Valente
lo que les dijo el licantropo / what the werewolf told them - Chely Lima
Greater Grave - Jacq Greyja
cyclorama - Davy Knittle

RECENT & FORTHCOMING
OS PRINT::DOCUMENTS and PROJECTS, 2019-20

2020

Institution is a Verb: A Panoply Performance Lab Compilation
Poetry Machines: Letters for a Near Future - Margaret Rhee
My Phone Lies to me: Fake News Poetry Workshops as
Radical Digital Media Literacy - Alexandra Juhasz, Ed.
Goodbye Wolf-Nik DeDominic
Spite - Danielle Pafunda
Acid Western - Robert Balun
Cupping - Joseph Han

KIN(D)* TEXTS AND PROJECTS

Hoax - Joey De Jesus
#Survivor - Joanna C. Valente
Intergalactic Travels: Poems from a Fugutive Alien - Alan Pelaez Lopez
RoseSunWater - Angel Dominguez

GLOSSARIUM: UNSILENCED TEXTS AND TRANSLATIONS

Zugunruhe - Kelly Martinez Grandal (tr. Margaret Randall)
En el entre / In the between: Selected Antena Writings -
Antena Aire (Jen Hofer & John Pluecker)
Black and Blue Partition ('Mistry) - Monchoachi (tr. Patricia Hartland)
Si la musique doit mourir (If music were to die) -
Tahar Bekri (tr. Amira Rammah)
Farvernes Metafysik: Kosmisk Farvelære (The Metaphysics of Color: A Cosmic
Theory of Color) - Ole Jensen Nyrén (tr. Careen Shannon)
Híkurí (Peyote) - José Vincente Anaya (tr. Joshua Pollock)

2019

Ark Hive-Marthe Reed
I Made for You a New Machine and All it Does is Hope - Richard Lucyshyn
Illusory Borders-Heidi Reszies
A Year of Misreading the Wildcats - Orchid Tierney
Of Color: Poets' Ways of Making | An Anthology of Essays on Transformative Poetics - Amanda Galvan Huynh & Luisa A. Igloria, Editors

KIN(D)* TEXTS AND PROJECTS

A Bony Framework for the Tangible Universe-D. Allen
Opera on TV-James Brunton
Hall of Waters-Berry Grass
Transitional Object-Adrian Silbernagel

GLOSSARIUM: UNSILENCED TEXTS AND TRANSLATIONS

Śnienie / Dreaming - Marta Zelwan/Krystyna Sakowicz, (Poland, trans. Victoria Miluch)
High Tide Of The Eyes - Bijan Elahi (Farsi-English/dual-language) trans. Rebecca Ruth Gould and Kayvan Tahmasebian
In the Drying Shed of Souls: Poetry from Cuba's Generation Zero Katherine Hedeen and Víctor Rodríguez Núñez, translators/editors
Street Gloss - Brent Armendinger with translations of Alejandro Méndez, Mercedes Roffé, Fabián Casas, Diana Bellessi, and Néstor Perlongher (Argentina)
Operation on a Malignant Body - Sergio Loo (Mexico, trans. Will Stockton)
Are There Copper Pipes in Heaven - Katrin Ottarsdóttir (Faroe Islands, trans. Matthew Landrum)

DOC U MENT

/däkyəmənt/

First meant "instruction" or "evidence," whether written or not.

noun - a piece of written, printed, or electronic matter that provides information or evidence or that serves as an official record
verb - record (something) in written, photographic, or other form
synonyms - paper - deed - record - writing - act - instrument

[*Middle English, precept, from Old French, from Latin documentum, example, proof, from docre, to teach; see dek- in Indo-European roots.*]

Who is responsible for the manufacture of value?

Based on what supercilious ontology have we landed in a space where we vie against other creative people in vain pursuit of the fleeting credibilities of the scarcity economy, rather than freely collaborating and sharing openly with each other in ecstatic celebration of MAKING?

While we understand and acknowledge the economic pressures and fear-mongering that threatens to dominate and crush the creative impulse, we also believe that ***now more than ever we have the tools to relinquish agency via cooperative means,*** fueled by the fires of the Open Source Movement.

Looking out across the invisible vistas of that rhizomatic parallel country we can begin to see our community beyond constraints, in the place where intention meets resilient, proactive, collaborative organization.

Here is a document born of that belief, sown purely of imagination and will. When we document we assert. We print to make real, to reify our being there. When we do so with mindful intention to address our process, to open our work to others, to create beauty in words in space, to respect and acknowledge the strength of the page we now hold physical, a thing in our hand, we remind ourselves that, like Dorothy: *we had the power all along, my dears.*

THE PRINT! DOCUMENT SERIES

is a project of

the trouble with bartleby

in collaboration with

the operating system

Printed in the USA
CPSIA information can be obtained
at www.ICGtesting.com
LVRC081638060823
754476LV00007B/116